POLITICS MOVES ONLINE

Old News: The Press and Politics in the 1990s, essays by Jay Rosen and Paul Taylor), and we examined the new technology that had suddenly burst on the scene—the World Wide Web. In Bill Kovach and Tom Rosenstiel's *Warp Speed,* we began to explore the impact the new technology could have on politics. While the Internet's place in the 2000 election campaign garnered a great deal of attention, its scope and nature was not clear, which is not surprising given how new the Internet is. This report is an attempt to understand exactly the difference online efforts made in both the 2000 and 2002 campaigns—and what it promises for the future.

In the pages that follow, Cornfield presents a baseline of information that will be invaluable to researchers in years to come. This report also helps us to understand some of the broader questions about the Internet's potential to revolutionize politics. On behalf of The Century Foundation, we thank him for this interesting and thoughtful analysis.

Richard C. Leone, President
The Century Foundation
November 2003

CONTENTS

PREFACE

The news in presidential politics early in the summer of 2003 caught many people by surprise. The leading candidate for the 2004 Democratic presidential nomination was an obscure former governor from a tiny state with a reputation for offbeat politics, a man with no personal fortune to spend and no organized or identity-based constituency to count on as a base of support. Howard Dean was nevertheless anointed by the national news media as a serious contender. Unlike Jimmy Carter, a candidate with a similarly slender political base, Dean had not prevailed in the Iowa caucuses to make the covers of *Time, Newsweek,* and *U.S. News & World Report.* That first vote in the race for convention delegates was still half a year away. Instead, Dean had finished ahead of his competitors in the "MoveOn.org primary" and "the money primary." Tens of thousands of his supporters were congregating at monthly "Meetups," and conversing in "discussion groups" and "blogs." Over a quarter of a million people had given the Dean campaign their "e-mail" addresses.

Blogs? MoveOn.org? As recently as a decade ago, these achievements would have struck even the most sophisticated observers of the race for the presidency as political science fiction. What they represent, instead, is the flowering of campaigning on the Internet, or online campaigning—the roots of which are described and analyzed in this book.

THE NET AND THE WEB

The Dean phenomenon cannot be fully appreciated without a somewhat arbitrary yet necessary distinction between "the Net" and "the Web." In common parlance, the two phrases are interchangeable. Many people also use the term "Web site" as a synonym for a campaign presence on the

Internet. Yet the Dean campaign Web site, www.deanforamerica.com, provides the slightest of clues to the campaign's success. It has the same format and kinds of information as the Web sites for Dean's competitors and, indeed, most campaign Web sites at the statewide or federal levels. But there is more to the Net than just the Web, let alone a particular Web site.

Focusing on a single Web site reflects a mass communications mentality oriented to the sequential consumption of individual media products. A book is a media product read from cover to cover; a television show is watched from start to finish; advertisements placed in a profusion of places and formats entice people to read the book and watch the show. Beginning, middle, end, go to the next one; beginning, middle, end, go to the next one: for people over thirty, this is a mass media consumption rhythm inculcated since early childhood. A newspaper, magazine, CD, or DVD comes closer to the Net/Web experience. These mass media products have numbered pages or segments that indicate a main sequence to be followed, but their modular structure permits consumption out of sequence.

In contrast, the ease with which Internet users flit from product to product, and from page to page within a product, suggests that understanding communications in this medium requires a reorientation. One must focus on the connections as much as the contents. The Internet, or Net, is an electronic platform for establishing social connections. Campaigns turn to the Net and the myriad of distribution channels, interactive forums, and message formats it houses—Web sites, yes, but also e-mail, instant messaging, discussion groups, blogs (a sort of diary that permits others to comment), pop-up advertisements, searchable databases, and so forth—in order to win an election. The more voters a campaign establishes connections with, the better it will fare. More important, in these early years of online campaigning, the more activists a campaign ensnares in its network-on-the-Net, the more money and volunteer hours it will collect, and the more voters it will be able to reach through mass media and physical contacts.

Like most campaign Web sites, Deanforamerica.com contains an assortment of promotional material, digital versions of the stuff that has lain on candidate display tables for decades. The first paragraphs of news releases and position papers run down the center column of the home page. Biographical material about the candidate and photographs from the campaign trail may be accessed from the left-hand column, while the right-hand column features sign-up boxes for petitions, volunteer work, contributions, and voter registration, along with a link to the online store where buttons and bumper-stickers may be purchased. None of this would startle the political sophisticate from the recent past. And none of it would knock an online campaign specialist, or dot-pol, for a loop. A dot-pol would regard much of Deanforamerica.com's contents as "brochure-ware," yesterday's formats transposed to today's new medium, vaudeville skits on television.

For an appreciation of the political power that the Dean campaign has extracted from its Internet presence, one must be alert to the structural significance of a quartet of simulated file folder tabs running along the top of the Deanforamerica.com home page. "Contribute" opens a virtual door to electronic donations, either on a one-time basis or through an installment plan that deducts a designated amount from a credit card account every month until the donor has reached the legal maximum. "Get Local" brings the site visitor to a database of upcoming campaign events, searchable within one hundred or the visitor's choice of miles from any zip code in the nation. This tab also features a toolkit to help volunteers plan events and a link to MeetUp.com, a company that uses the Internet to arrange monthly gatherings of people with common interests at coffeehouses, restaurants, and other public locales.

"DeanLink" provides a means for individuals to put together their own networks through e-mail, instant messaging, and dedicated pages on the Dean Web site. An imitation of Friendster, a commercial online dating service, DeanLink relies on the desire for social contact as a springboard to campaign involvement. Access is screened and monitored through password-entry software. The preeminent DeanLinker as of October 12, 2003, was Jonathan Kriess-Tomkins of Sitka, Alaska. The Web page about him provided links to pages about the 447 persons linked to the Dean campaign through him, a list of his interests, a link to his personal home page, and a photograph of him holding an ice-cream cone. (Jonathan is fourteen years old.)

"Official Blog" leads to blogforamerica.com, a parallel Web site to that of the campaign. The middle column contains diary entries from a handful of Dean campaign managers in reverse chronological order; the top entry is usually no more than a few hours old. A blog reader can send any entry to a friend, trace it back through preceding entries to which it is intimately related, or follow it through to comments posted by other readers. In this way, visitors to blogforamerica.com pick up threads of monologues and conversations, as though they were wandering through a campaign headquarters. The right column reprises calls to action posted on the regular campaign Web site and catalogs the blog entries by the time and day they appeared and by category. The left column consists of hundreds of links to Dean-related activity elsewhere on the Web, mostly run by supporters with no official ties to the campaign. Deanybopper clips articles from major newspapers. The Dean Defense Forces call talk shows and write editors to correct what they perceive as unfair coverage. Switch To Dean, imitating an advertising campaign of Apple Computer, collects and displays homemade Web videos with testimonials from erstwhile supporters of other candidates who have now committed to Dean. The Dean Corps puts volunteers to work in local communities in Iowa, cleaning up rivers and collecting supplies for schools and food banks.

Other campaigns have established similar features. But the Dean campaign has assembled by far the biggest and most active online campaign network. On October 15, 2003, according to the campaign, there were 466,884 people on the e-mail list, 123,331 had signed up to attend a Meetup, 78,330 had attended at least one of 6,177 events organized through the Get Local feature, and 168,000 had donated an average of $73.69 in the July–September 2003 quarter for a total of $14.8 million. That set a record for quarterly fund-raising by a Democratic presidential candidate, and brought the total raised in 2003 to $25.3 million. (In the same third quarter, the Bush reelection campaign raised $49.5 million and touted the 145,000 contributions of less than $200.)

The average amount of a Dean donation was as remarkable a tribute to the strength of his support network as the amount the campaign raised. According to the Campaign Finance Institute, 70 percent of all individual donations to major-party presidential candidates in the first nine months of 2003 came in contributions of $1,000 or more. The comparable statistic for 1999 was 67 percent. But Dean raised 55 percent of his millions in donations of $200 or less.[1] The Dean network also has contributed tactical intelligence. The campaign took the advice of a supporter in deciding to solicit handwritten letters from MeetUp attendees to uncommitted voters in Iowa and New Hampshire.

What this means in terms of delegates and votes remains to be seen. But Dean has used his online network to help him win at two new stops on the campaign trail, which also would not be conceivable without the Internet. The MoveOn.org primary was a straw poll staged by an online activist group described in Chapter 5. Dean won 139,360 votes, 44 percent of the total; more significant, he reaped 54,730 volunteer pledges, 49,132 financial pledges, and 77,192 additions to the campaign e-mail list. The money primary, detailed in the same chapter, is a veritable straw poll created by a confluence of online activities by political campaigns, journalists, and the Federal Election Commission.

Even if the Dean campaign sputters or collapses before Iowa, it has left a legacy for dot-pols. It has shown them, and the entire community of professional politics, that the experiments in online campaigning conducted around the turn of the millennium have borne fruit. For all campaigners, the year 2004 looms as the year 1 A.D.

PROFESSIONAL CAMPAIGNING

This report focuses on what campaigners in the United States did with the Internet in the years 1999–2002. By campaigners, I mean those who, in classic Weberian terms, live for or make a living off politics: candidates; issue advocates; government, party, and interest group officials, their staffs, and their consultants.[2] Those campaigners with a special interest in adapting the Internet to their work will be referred to as "dot-pols"; they are change agents who constitute a critical subset of the campaigning community. Online and off-line, campaigners initiate the bulk of political action in the public square, which elicits reactions from journalists, citizens, and policymakers. Policymakers are, of course, often the same people who campaign. But the two modes of operation are different and create dilemmas of priority. Whereas policymakers seek above all to govern, that is, to steer the ship of state on the basis of legal authority, collaborative negotiations, and deliberative dialogue, the primary objective of campaigners is to win an upcoming vote by an electorate, legislative, or other decisionmaking body.[3]

Since the late 1960s, campaigning has been increasingly dominated by a blend of marketing and military techniques known as the "professional" style. The professional campaign is by now distinctive and pervasive enough to be disparaged abroad as the "American" campaign. Its communicative core consists of for-hire specialists directing politicians in the repetition of carefully designed statements, or messages, to carefully specified audiences, or targets. The conventional channels for targeted messages are broadcast and cable television (the locus of the "air war"); rally sites, meeting halls, mall entrances, and residential doorsteps (the "ground war"); and radio, telephone, bulk or "direct" mail, and graphic displays (not called the "war at sea," but no less essential for lacking a metaphorically apt nickname).

Professional campaigners take an elaborate approach to political communication, known as message development. A message is the central rationale and motivation the public must accept in order for it to act as the campaign desires. It may be thought of as the words that complete the sentence that begins, "Vote for us because. . . ." Because it's the economy, stupid. Because we have a Contract with America. Because we'll build a bridge to the twenty-first century. Because if the glove don't fit, you must acquit. Because we are compassionate conservatives. Campaign professionals ask clients what they want and guide them in the articulation of a message that will win them the support they need to prevail with a decisionmaking body. Message development is not rocket science, but it is not as obvious as the best practitioners make it look, for it is embedded at every stage—research, creation, testing, and release—in complex, expensive, and customized uses of technology.

The consultants and staffers who direct the production and distribution of campaign communication are preponderantly white, male, young, well educated, and ideologically moderate.[4] They love the all-consuming, historically and ideologically tinged competition of politics, so much so that the most successful ones forgo or curtail steadier, more lucrative jobs in public relations and advertising, which campaigning resembles in many respects. There are fundamental differences though between selling candidates and selling cars. A campaigner's "products" need far more than market share to be considered successful, and they are not available for sale every day. The product features of politics consist of issue positions and character traits, which are harder to define than a commercial good. Like the car sellers, however, the basis of the campaigners' power resides in the perception among their clients that they possess expertise in how to use communications technologies in ambiguous and often volatile situations.

These political clients fall into two basic categories, according to their electoral or policy orientation. In the former, more visible category, campaign professionals are hired by candidates for office and the political parties that nominate and funnel money to them. In the latter, more stable category, corporations, interest groups, trade associations, unions, and coalitions thereof contract with campaign professionals to help them win a decision before a government body and, more generally, to "manage issues," that is, maintain a good public image with respect to affairs in which they have a stake. Issue management occurs every day of every year and sometimes consists of forestalling votes instead of trying to win them. So it comes as no surprise to learn which campaign category is larger: In 2000, approximately $4 billion was spent on electoral campaigns in the United States, $3 billion of it at the national level.[5] The

policy campaign market that year was estimated at $35 billion.[6] These fig-
ures may seem large. Campaign finance reformers often make them seem
so. But while the business of campaigning rose sharply during the 1990s,
it represents a mere 1–2 percent of the polling, advertising, telemarketing,
and public relations markets.[7]

Campaigners are not full professionals, like doctors, lawyers, and
architects. They do not need a license, verified mastery of a codified body
of knowledge, and pledged fealty to a code of ethics in order to sell their
services. Rather, like journalists, campaigners are semiprofessionals, in
that they are imbued with a sense of public service that complicates and
can even override their business commitments to their clients. It runs
against the popular stereotype to speak of campaign professionals as political idealists. But very few of them will work for very long on behalf of
clients who do not share their dreams for American politics. It is an un-
spoken and nearly unbreakable rule in the vocation that Democrats work
for Democratic clients and Republicans for Republican clients. Many policy consulting firms are bipartisan ventures, with a star from each party on
the nameplate to maximize the client list without violating the precept.

The Internet presented professional campaigners with a subtle and
sizable challenge. At first glance, the new communications technology
resembled many of the media channels and devices that campaigners
used to win votes and earn a living. A campaign Web site was like the
reception area of a headquarters, a place for brochures and other publicity
materials. The rest of the Web was analogous to a library in one sense,
and to a grid of streets and highways in another: the places where one did
research and put up billboards. E-mail was a fabulous melding of the
telephone, fax, and postal service. Instant or text messaging could be
understood as enhanced pagers. And computerized databases corre-
sponded to the file cabinets in the back of the headquarters.

But there the analogies ended. Each of these components of the
Internet were intimately connected through the electronic network. Each
could be used by many persons at every minute of the day from every spot
on earth, some accessing the system according to plan but some ran-
domly, some anonymously, and some surreptitiously. Messages could
move at the speed of light, and they could also stay within reach for
years. Connection lines, traffic patterns, and message components could
all be analyzed and automatically improved by computer programs. And
every day, it seemed, a better version of one aspect of the technology hit
the market, making it a constant effort to stay on the cutting edge and,
more important, to stay connected to as many people as possible.

The arrival of the Internet in American society thus meant several things at once to the professional politicking community. It was a threat to business as usual, an opportunity for new firms and new divisions of established firms, an unknown factor in an already complicated communications milieu, and an object of fashionable curiosity.

OVERVIEW

To determine what was happening in e-politics, I relied on journalism and word of mouth within the nascent online politics community to find the best instances of online campaigning that I could. I watched these campaigns from afar (the Internet was, of course, wondrously helpful on this score), read numerous periodicals, conducted more than fifty interviews, and attended dozens of meetings of online politickers. In my capacity as research director for the Democracy Online Project (now the Institute for Politics, Democracy, and the Internet), I commissioned and supervised a series of nine case studies of online campaigning in municipal elections in 1999, several surveys in the 1999–2002 time period, and a questionnaire for campaign managers in 2002. I have drawn on technology studies to give a sense of the range of possibilities for Internet use and upon social science to ferret out empirically unsupportable bits of conventional wisdom. I also have sought perspective from recent studies of professional campaigning.[8]

My methods and approach have limitations. Except for the survey research, I could not ascertain the representativeness of the evidence and testimony I encountered and collected. In "hanging out" with members of a community, I was susceptible to the biases attendant on "going native." However, if the objective is to take stock of online politics, one had better spend time watching and listening to those in the campaign vocation. They will have a greater say in determining the application of networked technology to this field than any other force, simply because they engage more in politics. For the same reason, they are critical in shaping how democratic the character of public discourse will be online.

The first chapter looks at how the late 1990s and early 2000s represented a time of discovery and experimentation in online campaigning. From the start of the World Wide Web, a few in the politics vocation began to fiddle with the technology, endeavoring to apply it to message development. By Election Day 2000, approximately one thousand people were working in online politics in the United States.[9] They had, by that biggest of "sale days," battle-tested some techniques that could be replicated, integrated, and applied to most election and advocacy campaigns.

Chapter 2 looks at research, the most common use of the Internet in online campaigning. The Internet brings a cornucopia of information to everyone connected to it, citizens as well as campaigners. However, the democratization of political research is not the revolutionary spark some might think. Because professional campaigners conduct more political research, of higher strategic quality, and in a timely fashion, they and their clients retain an edge in the political power that information can confer.

Chapter 3 explores campaign Web sites. Their properties are intrinsically fascinating and have received much attention from political observers because they are easily inspected. But professionals learned early on that a campaign Web site is only as useful as the publicity pathways built to it, as well as out from it. They also recognized the risks in posting information readily available to all for a long, long time. At the conclusion of this transitional phase, they sensed that solutions to the publicity and visibility problems of campaign Web sites might be found through better use of e-mail. But at that point, they had made limited progress in deploying e-mail to good effect.

The dismal state of online advertising helps explain this limited progress. Online advertising, both for sheer publicity and for raising money, languished in the period under study. Chapter 4 examines the perplexing interplay of obstacles retarding the growth of raising and spending campaign money online (advertising being a mainstay of campaign spending). It contends that the ultimate value of the Internet for exposure and fund-raising depends on the development of negotiating protocols, measurement formulas, message formats, and pricing mechanisms that political professionals, the advertising industry, the regulatory commissions, and the online public all can accept. The bet here is that campaign money will circulate as commonly online as it does off-line, but the set of standards and practices making that practical may be as much as a decade away.

Chapter 5 consists of case studies of online campaigning. The first reviews the growing sophistication that the Bush-Cheney campaign brought to its use of the Net in 2000. Next comes an analysis of the spectacular results of the McCain online campaign after the New Hampshire primary and of the less appreciated work that went into it. The third case study, probably the most important, details the innovative influence of MoveOn.org, the only online political entity to date to succeed twice at the national level. The next serves up lessons from the civic network Web White and Blue for online political debates and related campaign forums. Finally, the chapter offers reflections on online polls and ratings systems, and what they reveal about the potential of the Internet for direct democracy.

The concluding chapter takes stock of this transition period from several perspectives. It reviews speculative literature on online politics from the 1990s and contends that not much of what was forecast has been either confirmed or contradicted by the record to date. There is no revolution, but there is no triumph of the status quo, either. It analyzes the state of online politics from the perspective of technological diffusion theory. Finally, the chapter predicts that the Internet will become essential to successful campaigns for public support as a command-and-control center. Dot-pols will sit before a computer console through which all campaign communication will be integrated and fine-tuned. The advent of online campaigning makes clear that all successful campaigns are network-based; therefore, all campaigns should make use of the Internet.

ACKNOWLEDGMENTS

Much of the research for this report was funded by a grant from the Pew Charitable Trusts, which established the Democracy Online Project at the George Washington University Graduate School of Political Management, where I served as research director. I am grateful to Sean Treglia of Pew and F. Christopher Arterton of the Graduate School for underwriting my work. Thanks also go to Ruy Teixeira and Thad Hall of The Century Foundation for commissioning the report, to Julie King, Christine McConville, Akis Skertsos, and Ryan Thornburg for research assistance, to Thomas Mann and Joel Swerdlow for editorial suggestions, and to Beverly Goldberg and Steven Greenfield for patient and careful editing of the manuscript.

My parents, Dr. Maurice B. and Gloria Cornfield, passed away during the period explored in this work. Both cared about the quality of American politics. Neither ever went online. My son Matthew was born during this same time span; at two years old, he is already playing on Web sites. I suspect that these family events inclined me to emphasize the transitional aspects of online campaigning. To the extent that there is any stability in this account of a milieu where everything seems in motion, I owe that to my wife, Kathryn Mimberg.

1
INTERNET TIME

During the last days of the 2000 presidential campaign, a flurry of incidents signaled the arrival of online technology in mainstream American politics:

- In an ingenious end run around the major parties, several Web sites sprang up and offered to match supporters of Gore and Nader from strategically selected states. By consummating mutual promises to vote for their Net-partner's candidate, citizens could work to realize a scenario in which Gore would win the election and Nader's Green Party would attain 5 percent of the vote and be eligible for public funding in 2004.[1] Tens of thousands visited these "vote-trading" sites before several Republican secretaries of state moved to shut them down, squelching the experiment in distributed deal making.

- In a demonstration of both how important and how vulnerable online campaigning could become, on Election Day 2000 someone defaced one of the home pages of the Republican National Committee, and another intruder disrupted the e-mail system of the Democratic National Committee.[2] Both security breaches were repaired swiftly. However, both were easy fixes. Election Day looms as a plump target for online attacks since it lasts a short number of hours, and get-out-the-vote operations by campaigns during those hours can make a difference.

- The N.A.A.C.P. relied on the Net and sophisticated software to re-adjust the telephone calling schedules of its get-out-the-vote (GOTV) coordinators every thirty minutes, based on early returns in pivotal precincts. This system proved its worth when polling stations in

St. Louis were reopened late in the evening by court order. The cyber-network adjusted, contributing to (deceased) Missouri governor Mel Carnahan's narrow Senate victory over the incumbent, John Ashcroft.

- Early in the morning after Election Day, the Gore inner circle relied on the Net to learn that Bush's lead in Florida had collapsed from thousands to hundreds of votes, prompting the Democrat to reverse his concession and challenge the result. The Florida secretary of state's Web site posted real-time returns, in a sharp technological contrast to the performance of some of the state's voting machines.

- As the electoral dispute unfolded, partisans intent on collecting testimony from aggrieved Florida voters discovered that some of them had already posted complaints via e-mail. The Net had given citizens an easy way to bring problems to the timely attention of political authorities and advocates.

- The Internet also enabled political authorities and advocates to communicate among themselves more efficiently as a preface to concerted action. The transcontinental teams of lawyers assembled by Bush and Gore used the Net to research and write their court briefs. While they worked out of public view, an e-mail from a Chicago lawyer to thirty friends, urging them to "bombard the news media" with demands for a Gore concession, snowballed into thousands of messages in a few days' span to newspaper editors whose e-mail addresses were included in the lawyer's missive.[3] Some of these editors told their readers that the online lobbying did not affect their views of the election controversy. But these public denials were belied by their decisions to treat the "snowball" as news.

These political activities occurred at the end of a decade in which the Internet made its debut beyond narrow, specialized circles of Americans. A combination of economic, governmental, social, and technological forces drove the rapid diffusion of the new medium. The World Wide Web, a system for delivering and displaying multimedia documents on the network of computers known as the Internet, made its public debut in 1991, followed two years later by the appearance of Mosaic, a method to "browse" the Web. These innovations sparked interest in the Internet beyond its original users in academia and government.

In 1994, commercial sites arose online. The following year, the U.S. government turned much of the Net over to private businesses and consortia. That year, as civic activist Tracy Westen notes, three milestones were passed: Americans bought more computers than television sets, sent more e-mail (which does not require Web access and skills) than surface mail, and transmitted more data messages than voice messages.[4] Bill Gates noticed the trend and voiced his concerns in a memo about the threat posed to Microsoft by Netscape, the company that devised a popular Web browser. In 1996, the federal government deregulated telecommunications to spur competition for phone and cable service, two principal conduits of Internet traffic. Venture capital firms stepped up their staking of "Internet start-ups," to the point where the phrase became shorthand in the late 1990s for a voguish place to work. The Y2K scare punctuated the decade of the broad introduction of the technology, as fears of what would happen to computer networks and databases when some terminals failed to distinguish between 1/1/(19)00 and 1/1/(20)00 pushed many organizations to upgrade their computer equipment, thereby improving their access to the Internet.[5]

The world of campaigns, elections, and issue advocacy orbited far from the high-tech sun but still felt its pull. Dot-pols, campaigners with a special interest in the potential uses of the Internet in campaigns, emerged at the same time as digital communication pioneers focusing on other matters. In 1993, Ken Deutsch put a Web site together for the "Baby Bell" regional phone companies to advocate in the area of telecommunications policy. Dan Carol built the first campaign Web site, for California senator Dianne Feinstein, in 1994. Steve Clift and Scott Reents of Minnesota E-Democracy sponsored the first online candidate debates that year. In 1995, both Phil Gramm and Lamar Alexander laid claim to being the first presidential candidate to open a Web site. That same year, Phil Noble launched PoliticsOnline, a consulting firm that offered specialized news about online campaigning as well as software and services. Shabbir Safdar of Voters Telecommunications Watch teamed up with Jonah Seiger and Jerry Berman of the Center for Democracy and Technology and staged an online protest when the Communications Decency Act was signed into law in 1996.[6] Bob Dole, the Republican nominee in 1996, referred to the Web site that Robert J. Arena built for his campaign at the conclusion of the first presidential debate in the fall. Dole gave out a slightly incorrect Web address, yet the site recorded more than two million hits in the ensuing twenty-four hours.

These campaign firsts went largely unnoticed in the public square.[7] When Jesse Ventura won the 1998 Minnesota gubernatorial race as a third-party candidate, the three top U.S. newsweeklies lavished attention on the victor. But these bellwethers of the mainstream national media did not report on the role played by "the JesseNet," Ventura's online campaign operation, in the upset. In 1999, they tuned into the story. "In the ever-accelerating world of the Internet," wrote Howard Fineman in *Newsweek,* "e-campaigning has gone from novelty to necessity in less than a year."[8] By this time, Rebecca Fairley Raney (who did report on the JesseNet) had developed online campaigning into a beat for the *New York Times.* Two online publications, *Slate* and the *Industry Standard,* joined with reporters at the *Washington Post* to publish a frequent column called "Net Election." "Net Election" ran regularly in the three online outlets and occasionally in the print versions of the *Industry Standard* and the *Post.*

The surge of news media interest in online campaigning coincided with the apogee of the NASDAQ boom and the onset of the 2000 presidential race. On the sound logic that presidential election years are prime times to introduce new political products and services, dozens of online politics initiatives materialized in (or were beefed up for) the 2000 election cycle, which began in 1999. Political entrepreneurs, some with millions of dollars in venture capital stakes, counted on public predictions that 2000 would be "The Year of the Net" and publicized themselves through that slogan. But by the time of the Republican and Democratic conventions, it was clear that expectations would not be met. No speaker at either convention invited the television audience to visit a Web site. The only time George W. Bush referred to the Internet during his acceptance speech was to gibe at his opponent for being the reputed "father" of the medium. The line got a huge laugh, yet there was no concerted online follow-through. Al Gore did not attempt to refute or otherwise turn the tables on Bush. The online bubble, lacking news and political networking to sustain it, collapsed.

The protracted election dispute gave online public affairs companies, divisions, and projects one last shot at making good on the "Year of the Net" prediction. News media portals, notably CNN.com and MSNBC. com, enjoyed unprecedented traffic spikes in November 2000 as millions of people checked the sites throughout the deadlock for the latest numbers and commentary. Alas, history is merciless to those who peg political predictions to the calendar. The year 2000 became the Year of the Chad, not the Net.[9] The collapse of the NASDAQ spoiled the triumph of the news media portals, which had to lay off employees despite record volume. In a final and ironic rebuke to those who had banked on 2000 being the Year of the Net in public affairs, the cause of online voting was initially advanced by the breakdown of voting equipment in Florida, only to suffer a mighty setback. Companies vending online voting systems were confronted by opinion poll and expert panel majorities who questioned the security, equity, verifiability, privacy, and general rationale for their product.[10] The companies retreated and began to push computerized, but not online, equipment. VoteHere.Net changed its name to VoteHere, just as Grassroots.com, a political start-up, became Grassroots Enterprises.

THE SCOPE AND PACE OF CHANGE

So much, it would seem, for the prophecies of the Internet spurring great change at a dizzying pace. If there was a digital revolution going on, it was not triggering an upheaval in politics. The Internet was not used to shift power among nations, classes, social types, or age groups.[11] The Berlin Wall fell before, not after, the Web arose, with the help of the videocassette, satellite television, and the fax machine.

On a lesser but still significant level of change, the Internet cannot be associated with any shuffling of the issues on the national public affairs agenda. It is true that, because of the Internet, more Americans express concern about corporations and governments gathering personal information without their permission and about the commercial and pornographic solicitations that appear, unbidden, on their computer screens. But Net-stimulated privacy concerns have yet to crystallize into a political movement on the scale of, say, abortion, guns, taxes, or the environment, issues candidates ignore at their peril. Using still another dimension of change, it would be an exaggeration to claim that online campaigning tipped the presidential election or any other contest in 2000, with the possible exception of the Missouri Senate race.

Yet, if the forecasters made a mistake in the 1990s, it was one of proportion, not direction. American politics has irreversibly crossed an important threshold. The race for the presidency is the most prominent political process in the world, a floodlighted and often supercharged sequence of events that brings special attention to campaign practices. Many people saw for the first time in 2000 how the Internet can work in politics. They did not have to be among the 102 million Americans with Internet access at that time to do so, since Internet politics was covered as a story in off-line media. However, increasing numbers of Americans have learned about online campaigning through direct experience.

What one may label the "online citizenry," an intersecting subset of the online and adult populations, continues to expand. More Americans are turning to the Internet for news or information about politics. The ranks of this online citizenry increased while the high-tech economy boomed and even after it collapsed, during midterm as well as presidential election years. In the summer of 2000, approximately 33 million Americans viewed political information online. In November 2002, the population of the online citizenry stood at 46 million. There is little reason to expect a reversal of this trend. Its primary propellants—the increased sophistication of Net users, the spread of broadband (high-speed, high-volume connections), and the periodic eruption of big news stories—do not need more technological breakthroughs and subsequent sales hype to be sustained.[12]

What has the online citizenry seen? And what has it done politically, the Internet being a medium for campaign action as well as news and education? The Internet has had an impact on voting and persuasion, the two activities most people associate with conventional politics. In 1998, 34 percent of the online public said that information it received about the elections through the Internet swayed the decision to vote for or against a particular candidate; in 2000, 43 percent said it had been so influenced, and the comparable figure was 25 percent in 2002.[13] It is hard to discern a trend in these numbers, especially given the ever-expanding population from which they are drawn. It is impossible to tie the survey data to an electoral contest, or group of contests, or segment of the electorate where the influence has been most acute. But it is undeniable that the Internet has become part of the media mix that animates politics.[14]

Meanwhile, on the supply side, dot-pols have begun to incorporate the Internet into the myriad of campaign activities in which politicians engage as they seek public support for elections and policies: research, publicity, advertising, press relations, organizational management, fundraising, volunteer recruitment, and volunteer/voter mobilization. The potential applications are as wide as can be imagined. Because the Internet supports mass communication (few-to-many), interpersonal communication (few-to-few), and interactive communication (many-to-many), there is scarcely an aspect of campaigning that cannot be conducted through it. Kissing babies does come to mind as an exception.

Technologically inspired political change may not be occurring on "Internet time," as the 1990s buzz term put it. There has been no shake-up in the distribution of political power. Nevertheless, the scope of Net adoption is comprehensive: from protesters to public relations, from zoning commissions to presidential races, from the momentarily curious and concerned to those who strive with every waking breath to have a successful career in public life. The Internet's time has, in fact, arrived in politics.

2
RESEARCH, REVOLUTION, REVELATION

A SMART-VOTER REVOLUTION?

The Internet is an incomparable technology for research. There is no quicker nor more economical way for one person to collect information on a topic than to go online. Sometimes information *arrives* faster and less expensively via other media, as when big news breaks and someone yells to go turn on the television. On September 11, 2001, 81 percent of Americans got most of their information from television, and there was no statistical difference between Internet users and nonusers in their reliance on TV news.[1] However, the Internet is now the single best method to collect information on a specific topic. The Web places at one's fingertips an expanding galaxy of stories, documents, discussions, tutorials, bulletins, databases, and, critically, indexes to all of the above. Increasingly, these come in audio and visual as well as textual and numerical forms. The experience of zooming through this galaxy via hyperlinks may be the Web's most arresting feature.

Beyond its telecommunications properties, the Web shrinks two steps in the research process to the vanishing point. First, a Web site may sport a good directory of resources, "good" in this context meaning comprehensive and current. Second, the linked-to resources (both on-site and elsewhere on the Web) may be organized into databases searchable by key words. The advent of good directories and searchable databases has transformed a process renowned for its tediousness into something much more palatable to members of a society addicted to instant gratification, to say nothing of saved transportation costs. By October 2001, the nonpareil search engine Google was servicing 130 million research requests a day.[2]

By the end of 2002, two-thirds of Americans (including those who went online rarely or not at all) told survey researchers that they expected to find information about health care, government services, and commercial products, as well as news online—and of those who went looking, more than 70 percent had their expectations met.[3]

During the 1990s, a constellation of Web sites materialized to help researchers get quick fixes on political contests.[4] Some of these repositories were built by familiar political, governmental, and journalistic institutions, such as the Republican National Committee, the Federal Election Commission, and the *Washington Post*. Some, such as Congress.org, PoliticsOnline.com, and (the now defunct) Voter.com, were "political portals," aspiring to dominate what they envisioned as a new niche market. The portals acted as a clearinghouse for details that politicos needed to know in order to make use of such online tools as fund-raising programs and e-mail forms to fill out and send to decisionmakers. Nonprofit organizations, such as the California Voter Foundation (www.calvoter. org) and Project Vote Smart (www.vote-smart.org), procured and aggregated online information intended to help citizens make well-informed choices at the polls. Campaigns built their own Web sites, which will be examined in the next chapter. And individuals such as Alex Clemens transposed the political newsletter format onto the Internet; Clemens's Web site "The Usual Suspects" (now at www.sfpolitics.com) has since 1995 compiled and commented on political news of San Francisco with a raffish attitude.

Most of these Web sites were designed with the spectators of politics more in mind than its protagonists. The dot-com (for-profit) sites tried to make money by marketing themselves to political advertisers as a venue where they could reach the people who follow politics. The dot-orgs (nonprofits) sought to have a salutary impact on the democratic process by widely distributing political information and First Amendment action tools, that is, online ways of speaking, publishing, petitioning, and assembling in public. The debut of these sites thus raised anew the possibility of a surge in citizen participation in conventional politics. What would happen if millions of spectators, bulked up into casual researchers by the Net, entered the sound stages of politics, equipped with resources previously available in a timely fashion only to a few? Would these smart voters (and advocates) foist different scripts and directions on politicians? Would the Establishment crumple for want of control over the information through which political decisions were publicly legitimated? In health care, the stock market, and the music industry, individuals used the Internet in the late 1990s to circumvent institutions, find like-minded individuals, and challenge authority.[5] Why not in politics?

The most general source of resistance militating against a revolution of smart voters has to do with the nature of information. A cliché bids us to equate information with power, but that is not the case online, or anywhere else for that matter. Information empowers only when it answers questions on the minds of persons about to make a decision. I can post the time a soccer match starts in Stuttgart, but that information is useless to you if you are not interested in going to the match, you are unable to get to the stadium, the posting is out of date, or you do not understand German. The power of information, in other words, is contingent on the degree to which it helps people make choices by telling them about the likely consequences of actions they are currently considering. Information has impact to the extent it provides and catalyzes intelligence.[6] The "Information Revolution" is thus not analogous to previous technological revolutions. Having more information does not necessarily confer more power, as was generally the case with fire, steam, electricity, and nuclear fission.

Political information also has some peculiar characteristics that work against a smart-voter revolution. Americans are markedly less than satisfied with what they can learn about the political world through the Internet.[7] In campaigns, as elsewhere, the Internet has streamlined the pace and expanded the scope of research. But the inherent indeterminancy and contestedness of campaign information makes political research a tougher row to hoe than other fields. If I want to buy a stock, learn how to remove a carpet stain, report a broken streetlight, or find out who is at bat in a baseball game two thousand miles away, I can go online and get the information I want and in some instances accomplish what I want to do with the information. The research process I follow in each case may have some bewildering twists and hairpin turns. Still, the information I collect will, in all likelihood, not be subject to contemporaneous dispute, as it would if I wanted to figure out whom to vote for in the next election or which bill currently before the legislature merits my support. There will be Democratic, Republican, and news media versions of such seeming matters of fact as whether proposed legislation cuts taxes, shifts taxes, cuts the growth rate of taxes, and so forth. Advocates of each version will attack one another, sometimes in harsh and personal terms.

And then there is the question of effectiveness. Suppose I am interested in a political contest, and I resolve the factual ambiguities sufficiently to choose intelligently. If my goal is to decide how to vote, I am set. But if my goal is to elect someone I deem the better candidate, I am a lone voter in a big electorate. My capacity to carry out the objective depends in large part on others acting in concert with me and defeating opposing coalitions. Not exactly fixing a streetlight (although in some communities that is no easy task to accomplish, either).

These considerations make a smart-voter revolution a long shot. Nevertheless, two aspects of the contemporary political environment lend credence to a scenario in which Net-aided democratization of research supplies the wedge for a shake-up in American politics. The first is that a large segment of the electorate now calls itself independent. Between 1982 and 2000, 9–12 percent of Americans said they were independents and not Democrats or Republicans; expand the question to include the options of "Independent Democrat" and "Independent Republican" and the range leaps to 30–40 percent in the same time period.[8] The better-educated individuals who lived up to these independent identifications are prone to conduct research as discerning consumers of a new product do: absent brand loyalty, they are on the lookout for the candidate who offers them the best "value," as evident from the information they acquire. The second favorable condition is the state of parity between the two major parties, in both popular support and offices held at the national and state levels. Party parity, institutionalized through winner-take-all elections and computer-aided redistricting, has reduced the number of independents needed to tip the balance in political struggles. Consequently, a few smart voters could make a big difference in elections and policies. Was that not one of the lessons of the 2000 presidential election?

The best single Web site for a smart voter to bone up on an impending election is, appropriately enough, Project Vote Smart (PVS), at www.vote-smart.org. Since 1992, when it relied mainly on an 800 phone number and pamphlets, this civic organization has assiduously pursued the progressive vision of a nation of rational political agents who examine the facts and then act on them in a way that transcends partisanship, as calculators of their own and the public's best interests. That is "progressive," lower-case, in the procedural sense of the term; PVS is so strict about the appearance of bias that it says it would publicly condemn any candidate—including one who espoused Progressive views—who used its name in a campaign.

Using the most objective methods imaginable, Vote Smart compiles five interlocking databases for voters' consideration about candidates for state and federal office: contact and biographical information; an annotated record of critical votes taken by those candidates who have held legislative office; campaign finance information; interest group ratings; and responses to a questionnaire called the National Political Awareness Test (NPAT). The National Political Awareness Test, available for public inspection on the Web site, is sent to candidates who qualify for general elections. It is an education to read it, even without answers. It asks only what candidates are for, not against, which may seem Pollyannaish but cuts down on the strutting and demagoguery. For each issue area, there are multiple options reflective of the policy choices officials face. Budget and spending questions solicit answers along a six-point scale, from "greatly increase" to "eliminate." Perceptive readers are able to see who is unwilling to make hard choices from the pattern of answers. The 2002 NPAT for congressional candidates had 207 spaces to be filled out, including open-ended options for each of the twenty-one issue areas and the following short essay question: "On an attached page, in a total of seventy-five (75) words or less, please explain what your top two or three priorities will be if elected. Please explain how you would obtain any additional funding needed to implement these priorities."

Campaigns avoid questionnaires like biotoxins. They do not like to be pinned to a policy position, especially one framed by an outsider's concepts and words. In 2000, 4,802 of 12,510 candidates filled out the NPAT form. They were mostly also-rans, and their numbers are declining.[9] PVS attempts to coax answers out of candidates, enlisting news media organizations and local leaders. It also resorts to shaming. In 2000, PVS filled out NPATs for Bush and Gore on the basis of public statements, acridly noting in red ink, "On 31 separate occasions 17 national leaders from politics, journalism and political science contacted [the nominee] over an 11 week period, each requesting that [he] do the right and honorable thing by providing citizens with this critical information in the national interest." Similar red-ink entries greet visitors to Web pages for other candidates who duck the NPAT. This illustrates the main bias of the seemingly unbiased PVS: not to answer the questionnaire is to be in the wrong. However, PVS does advise voters that "if a candidate does not select a response to any part or all of any question, it does not necessarily indicate that the candidate is opposed to that particular item."

Assume, for the sake of the smart-voter scenario, that a torrent of publicity and public-spiritedness spurred ten million Americans to visit the PVS Web site. Assume that a preponderance of candidates took the test or had it taken for them by an expanded PVS corps. (PVS runs an internship program similar to the Peace Corps, with shorter terms of service.) Finally, assume that site visitors could discern the right choice for themselves through a fair and thorough sifting of the data. That likelihood could be enhanced by providing smart voters with their own issue position form to fill out and a software program to correlate their answers with the candidate databases so as to yield a compatibility ranking of all the candidates on each voter's ballot. SelectSmart.com (no connection to Project Vote Smart) offered such a service in 2000 for the presidential race and has one up for 2004.

The result would be a cadre of smart voters. Some of them might be moved to join the activists who participate in campaigns. Were they to materialize, there would be a basis for a progressive-style revolution in American politics.[10] But it would only be a basis, and a shaky one at that. In most cases, the professionals would outsmart the voters.

PROFESSIONAL POLITICAL RESEARCH

Campaigners differ from smart voters in how they approach the process of research. Vocational incentives impel campaign researchers to find information they and others on the team can use to win. They pay for access to exclusive online content, and they combine what they find online with information acquired through other channels. They write research reports on deadline. And they hone the messages they send (which compete with the PVS databases for voters' attention and allegiance) according to long-standing principles of strategy and rhetoric. In short, professionals apply stricter templates than citizens to the political information that crops up on their screens.

Political researchers pan for informational nuggets in three types of streams: personal, policy, and audience. Classicists will recognize that these research streams correspond to the exalted trinity of persuasive considerations in Aristotle's *Rhetoric*: ethos (the character of the speaker), logos (the logic of the case), and pathos (the mood of the audience). To win votes, campaigns seek to demonstrate that their side possesses the superior candidate, the stronger argument, and the better feel for what constituents care about. So it is only natural that they hunt for and display information that bolsters their candidates and causes.

PERSONAL RESEARCH

The Internet has created a windfall for campaign researchers specializing in the assembly of personal dossiers. The most notorious investigators compile incriminating dossiers on candidates and other public figures whom their clients oppose. That is why their specialty is known as opposition research. But professionals also conduct personal research on their own candidates and on other figures who come to public notice in the course of an election or policymaking battle.

Dossiers go well beyond the biographical information posted by campaigns and public sites such as Project Vote Smart. Online databases contain readily accessible records of an individual's financial, legal, medical, and residential movements (you never know what a former neighbor might have to say). Software programs record and retrieve an individual's online movements and multimedia appearances: sites visited, e-mails sent and received, camera lenses passed by, microphones approached.

"There is always something," Willie Stark tells Jack Burden, the opposition researcher who is the protagonist in Robert Penn Warren's novel *All the King's Men*. Today, if some item puts a celebrity in a nasty light, it may well wind up in the mischievous Web depository named after a Watergate-era phrase, www.thesmokinggun.com. This site presents what campaign researchers have chosen to bring to light. Visitors in the year 2000 could see in its archive the arrest record card filled out in Maine for George W. Bush in 1976, when the future Republican nominee was cited for driving under the influence of alcohol. A few entries down the index from that document sat a link to a facsimile of a North Carolina speeding ticket issued in 2000 to Al Gore's seventeen-year-old son, Albert. "The Smoking Gun" is not the worst of it; other sites and countless e-mails hurl rumor and innuendo into the public square. The most robustly vicious sites today post vitriol from angry customers and (ex-)employees of corporations, often at www.[corporation name here]sucks.com. Politicians are advised to purchase the domain name with the -sucks suffix before their enemies do. But, as will be seen in the account of the Bush for President campaign in Chapter 5, it is a futile exercise.

ISSUE RESEARCH

Policy researchers look for data, documents, and arguments bolstering issue positions that, when adopted by the campaign, will advance a contrast regarded as favorable to their candidates. At www.FedStats.gov, for example, a policy researcher can find a wide array of government statistics broken down state by state and sometimes by smaller geographic units. Such comparative data helps flesh out those "we are being denied our fair share of highway funds" and "we rank forty-ninth among the states in air quality" arguments so common to campaign cross fire. But policy researchers need not limit themselves to raw materials. Every think tank (and, it seems, nearly every professor conducting research of relevance to public affairs) has a Web site bulging with issue positions for politicians to adopt; www.townhall.com links to conservative policy reports, while www.movingideas.org does the same for liberals.

All this is grist for the briefing books campaigns put together to prepare candidates for debates and private meetings with potential endorsers. There is another kind of policy research common to campaigns that amounts to a kind of personal investigation in that it details the policy implications of an opponent's poor behavior: missed votes, "out of step" votes (that is, against the president, the party, the state delegation), squandered taxpayer dollars, "repaid" special interest contributions, and so forth. Much of this policy/personal hybrid research could be conducted by smart voters, as the information is in the public domain. But it takes too much time and concentration for it to be worthwhile to anyone except professionals, students of politics, and journalists.

The Center for Responsive Politics' www.opensecrets.org has done these researchers a great favor. It culls financial disclosure data from the Federal Election Commission (FEC) and organizes it for visitors so as to advance the case for campaign finance reform, articulated explicitly elsewhere on the site. A zip code entry box yields local angles on donors and recipients. E-mail newsletters and alerts suggest analytic pieces describing the money-in-politics angle on current issues (homeland security, prescription drugs, trade promotion authority). Most impressively, the Web site has a database that sorts ten years of political action committees (PACs) and individual contributions into 122 categorical blocks that suit the headlines: "Abortion: Pro-Choice," "Abortion: Pro-Life," "Accountants," and so forth.

Before the Internet, the Center published *Open Secrets* as a biannual book, eighteen months after the campaign cycle to which its data referred, at $200 a copy, with only two of its thirteen hundred pages allocated to financial data about each congressional incumbent.[11] Now that the database is online, the news media and political researchers can turn campaign contribution patterns into a news release, a news story, or even an issue for candidates to wrestle with. Opensecrets.org is by far the most popular database Web site among political reporters.[12]

AUDIENCE RESEARCH

The Web houses data from opinion polls and focus groups. There are some excellent civic sites, such as www.pollingreport.com, www.people-press.org, and www.publicagenda.com (which also presents policy research). Too often, however, what passes in public for audience research abandons the search for truth or subordinates it to the goals of entertainment, advertising, and persuasion. Methodological detail is a telltale sign of serious inquiry. The Internet creates abundant space for a survey group to post such essential details as question wording and order, cross-tabulations of results by (target group) categories, and comparable results from previous and simultaneous polls. When these details are absent, discerning researchers turn a deaf ear to the trumpeted results.

The Net not only can display audience research; it can be used to conduct it as well. The medium offers tantalizing potential: it is both less intrusive and more deliberative than telephone or face-to-face interviewing. But online surveys currently have the problem of devising a representative sample from a medium with only 60 percent penetration in the populace. Also, the absence of live interaction means that a respondent's lies, ironies, fantasies, mistakes, and other nuances may go undetected by survey administrators. Online focus groups, with or without videoconferencing, must grapple with a similar loss of interpretable body language. To serious researchers, then, online polling must be consumed carefully. In private, while deliberating strategy and tactics, political professionals are among those careful consumers; in public, they sometimes abandon those standards, as the last case study presented in Chapter 5 demonstrates.

"WORD-GATE" AND METARESEARCH

A fourth category of research suggests itself on the basis of an incident in the 2000 Minnesota Senate race, and that is Metaresearch. Because leaving a trail is the default condition of online activity, political researchers are increasingly susceptible to becoming a campaign issue themselves. This came to light in the unfolding of "Word-Gate," a Net-centric scandal that ensnared Senator Rod Grams in 2000 and may have contributed to his defeat.[13]

In May of that year, more than one hundred members of the Democratic-Farmer-Labor (DFL) Party received an e-mail from a "Katie Stevens," who described herself as a fellow progressive. Her missive attacked Mike Ciresi, one of four candidates for the DFL nomination to oppose Grams that fall. The attack was based on solid opposition research: it quoted Ciresi disparaging Paul Wellstone, the state's other senator and a DFL stalwart, and described cases that Ciresi's law firm had taken on behalf of corporate polluters. Three more e-mails ensued. But, despite e-mail correspondence and scheduled meetings, "Katie Stevens" could not be located by curious recipients of her messages. Then a Ciresi staffer clicked "File, Properties, Summary" on a Microsoft Word attach-ment to one of the e-mails. The name of Grams's opposition research director appeared in the author box.

Ciresi filed a complaint under Minnesota's Fair Campaign Practices Act, which makes it a felony to disseminate campaign information anony-mously. At the end of August, prosecutors went to the home of Grams's chief of staff, Christine Gunhus, whose name also appeared in the files, and seized two computers and nine diskettes. Word-Gate lost steam after Ciresi lost in the DFL primary, and Grams lost the general election to Mark Dayton. However, Gunhus, who pleaded no contest to a misde-meanor in 2001, had by that date married Grams.

PATTERN RECOGNITION

Were Willie Stark to be brought into the digital age, he might update his maxim about original sin and politics. Today, there is still "always something" of use to a campaign seeking advantages against rivals. There is always something on the dirt seeker and dirt finder, too—just as there turned out to be in the denouement to *All the King's Men*. The difference may lie in the digital nature of the "something" that the elec-torate may find persuasive. "The Smoking Gun" and Word-Gate notwith-standing, today's decisive evidence in politics and public affairs may take the form of a pattern of information (or, on the recursive, "meta-" level, a pattern of information circulation) instead of a single incriminating document.

Campaign researchers will find the Internet amenable to collecting data on the scale appropriate to their topics, whether examining personal files, policy briefs, or audience surveys. They will be wise to document their own searches, on the understanding that their sources and methods could become part of any dispute. They will use computers to detect and confirm patterns of behavior about which timely inferences can be made and will present their research graphically (moving beyond the ubiquitous PowerPoint format, one hopes).

A shining example of computer-assisted political research surfaced in March 2002, when a team of statisticians and sociologists from the American Association for the Advancement of Science testified in the war crimes trial of Slobodan Milosevic. The team analyzed data drawn from Albanian border guard registries, exhumation records, and interviews conducted by human rights activists. It argued that these sources showed that Yugoslav forces, not the Kosovo Liberation Army or NATO air attacks, were responsible for the refugee flows and killings in Kosovo in 1999.[14] The Internet did not have a direct role in this event. However, the Internet enabled the team to put the evidence and testimony into the global public square directly, completely, and undeniably. Cases such as this have buoyed the hopes of civic idealists everywhere that the Internet can transform the "information is power" equation into a force for enlightenment and justice.

REVELATORY DATABASES AND GRASSROOTS CAMPAIGNING

This chapter has placed citizens and professionals in counterpoint, but grassroots campaigners sometimes rely on political research to bring them together. When information comes as a revelation to a decision-making body—be it an electorate, Congress, jury, editorial board, president, or even the general public—the surprise can galvanize a change in anticipated outcomes. On such occasions, the research behind the revelation can be justly said to have been influential. For centuries, awareness of this dynamic has inspired political organizations to hire scandalmongers, whose craft embraces stroking cultural anxieties with rumors as well as with solidly grounded facts.[15] But the contingent nature of informational power remains applicable. If the breaking news a campaign circulates is regarded (or re-spun) as no big deal to the decisionmakers, then the revelation subsides into a momentary sensation, and nothing comes of the shock.

The Internet created a new setting for political revelation. Matt Drudge proved that. People no longer need to be present in the same room, or seated in front of the television set at the same time, or affiliated with the same organization, to be persuaded and mobilized. They do not even have to encounter the same information in order to react similarly and power a campaign. They just have to visit the same database.

No political entity has understood this better than the Environmental Working Group (EWG), a Washington, D.C.-based nonprofit research organization. Its signature has been the timely promulgation of extensive databases through which disparate people can find localized information that brings the outrageous consequences of a policy home to them. The Gore 2000 presidential campaign consulted www.ewg.org as the candidate traveled, inserting local details into their candidate's stock speech. An EWG Farm Subsidy Database, six years in the making, rattled the defenders of the nation's farm subsidy policy in early 2002 by making it possible for constituents to see how much money their neighbors had received from the government. Months later, EWG put together a database on behalf of a coalition opposing shipment of nuclear wastes to Yucca Mountain, Nevada. Visitors to the database could enter their street address and see how close they lived to a train or highway route that would be used to ship the waste. Insiders say this interactive map made the Senate vote closer, as non-Nevadans were moved to contact their statewide representatives to complain.

Both the farm subsidy and Yucca Mountain bills passed despite EWG's efforts. Perhaps the campaigns lost on their presentation of the case or perhaps through being on the short end of the apportionment of such other political resources as money, connections, and the existing structures of law and government. Regardless, the revelatory database is a new tool in politics. Like a charismatic figure, revelatory information shrewdly displayed online can inspire and guide individuals into political action. People can find the database through buzz; grassroots organizers can then aggregate their reactions and launch their comments and dollars at pivotal decisionmakers. In this way, citizens may be tapped as political extras: players in the process whose temporary presence in the right numbers at the right times and places could make a difference in a political struggle. Even when "wised up" by revelatory information and rounded up by campaigns, extras are not going to behave as effectively as professionals. Like their counterparts in movie epics, they add texture but do not drive the plot. They are there to be part of something big, not to display independence in action.

A revolutionary theory of online politics projects greater popular involvement in politics out of the notion that because more people *can* see more information in time to act on it, they *will*, and their efforts will be decisive. If men (and women) were smart voters, no campaigning would be necessary. Although the Internet makes it easier for individuals to act on what they see, it does not revise what Mancur Olson postulated as the logic of collective action: "rational, self-interested individuals will not act to achieve their common or group interests" unless the number of individuals is quite small or "unless there is coercion or some other special device."[16]

The Net is, in some respects, that special device. It makes easier the work of grassroots organizers in trying to overcome the inertia attributed to the logic of collective action. In their digital-era reconsideration of Olson's theory, Arthur Lupia and Gisela Sin conclude that, "by increasing noticeability, decreasing organization costs, or increasing the range over which credible commitments are possible, evolving technologies can transform formerly unattractive partners into attractive ones."[17] But the Net is not so special as to eliminate the need for organizers. Someone still has to come up with the revelation.

The track record and vocational predisposition of professional political researchers suggest that they are going to find revelatory information first and make the most and best use of it in the digital era. Opposition researchers will notice when something is missing from the dossier anyone can compile on a political figure, will investigate, and will intuit the revelatory value of what they discover. Issue researchers will recognize influential or insightful authors in the policy world and pay special attention to their work as it appears, thereby gaining an edge in ascertaining the political significance of a revelation. Pollsters, being familiar with panel data, measurement errors, sampling errors, and nonattitudes, will know when and how to discount some of the audience research they see, and thereby will locate those segments of a population most likely to be mobilized by certain types of knowledge.[18] And every research specialist with political experience will bear in mind that certain types of information absolutely essential to strategic intelligence will not be found online, except by mistake, as in Word-Gate.[19]

Short of revolution, absent cleverly packaged revelations, politics will yet be served well to the extent that high standards of documentation and presentation become the norm in online campaign research. Political education is a public good in its own right. The more that spectators, "extras," and professional players can know, the better the outcome. A high standard means disclosing sources, sponsors, and methods along with findings. It means providing as much context as possible. Hyperlinks allow these standards to be met with a little effort and minimal expense, depriving the lazy and feckless of an excuse. Early academic research suggests that the payoff in terms of public credibility to those who document their sources and methods will be substantial.[20] Precisely because the Net lends itself to research, having begun as a network for scholars, research standards have a foothold in this medium that they never enjoyed with older telecommunications channels. TheSmokingGun.com may not provide a platform for a smart-voter revolution, but it does not tell a lie.

CAMPAIGN WEB SITES AND PUBLICITY PATHWAYS

C ampaigns feed on publicity, the calling of attention to their appeals for support. The novelty of the Web site as a form of expression attracted sufficient attention in the mid-to-late 1990s to suggest that constructing one for a campaign might be a good publicity vehicle. At the least, a campaign could get a news story about its entry into the digital age of communication. By the 2000 cycle, the publicity limitations of the Web site had become apparent, and the novelty value was ebbing. However, political professionals hit on a publicity strategy that could compensate for those limitations. In essence, they came to regard a campaign Web site as the intermediate stop in a three-part communications process, the hub of a network of pathways along which their message could become better known.

Some of these pathways banked on advertising, described in the next chapter. Other pathways relied on adjusting candidate appearances so that they would be Net-friendly. But the key to the publicity process was e-mail. E-mail is, to date, the most valuable channel of communication the Net offers to campaigners. It pulls people into the campaign Web site and pushes into action those Web site visitors who have consented to give the campaign their e-mail address.

WELCOME TO MY WEB SITE

A campaign Web site is a dynamic but passive publicity device.[1] Its pages and links may—and should—change, but it cannot attract attention in and of itself. The only place in everyday life people can see a campaign

23

Web site is in front of a computer monitor. Not only must they choose to go there, they must know how to find it, an ancillary action much easier today than during the 2000 cycle. (Directory services and social knowledge of them are two developments that have, indeed, advanced in "Internet Time.") Web sites cannot be dropped on doorsteps, glimpsed from cars, or handed out in churches. But if Web sites lack the visibility of display graphics, Web site addresses can be placed on those graphics. That is why the first step in a good publicity strategy involves disseminating the campaign Web site address by all means possible, online and otherwise.

Internet-savvy consultants advised campaigns to treat their Web site addresses as though they were part of the campaign's name. Candidates should invite people to visit the site in every speech; receptionists (live and taped) should refer callers there for basic information; everyone affiliated with the campaign should collect e-mail addresses and so obtain tacit permission to send an e-mail message with a request to click on the link to the Web site. Search engines were to be apprised of the Web site address as early as possible and even to be paid fees for prominent placement on the list of sites returned when certain key words were entered. The digital property rights to cognate names (including [candidate's name] sucks) were to be purchased and "pointed" toward the Web site. Advertisements and display graphics should carry the Web site address as a matter of course.

In practice, most campaigns in 2000 did not tout their Web sites so extensively. The record improved slightly in 2002. More bumper stickers sported the URL (an acronym for Uniform Resource Locator, the technical term for a Web site address), and more television ads flashed the URL at the ad's conclusion. At least one campaign incorporated its Web site address into its official name: billchoby.org (Bill Choby ran for Congress in Pennsylvania). But the simple, inexpensive, and valuable idea that a URL ought to run for the entire duration of a television advertisement, much as television networks keep their logos visible at the bottom right-hand corner of the screen during programming, had yet to penetrate the campaign community.

What is so valuable about a campaign Web site? Studies show that when people alight on one, they will stay for as long as twenty minutes. Even half that time is a good long stretch in a milieu geared to handshakes and sound bites. It is time enough for people to get a solid sense of what a campaign stands for, who works on it, and what is its intended course of public action. It is time enough for campaigns to make an intelligent case and procure a commitment of support, one that in some respects can be converted on the spot into action. A campaign Web site, in short, is a rarity in the contemporary world, a place where politicians can recruit and mobilize volunteers by example, openness, wit, and instruction.

On the other hand, studies also show that some people spend long periods of time on a Web site because they do not know where to go next or how to get to a desired location. Finding one's way through a Web site can be like walking through a life-size maze, except that there are many more intersections and more options at each intersection. Web site design has emerged as an occupational niche to alleviate this problem. Yet, since people usually view Web sites inside the frame of a software program with its own options arrayed along the top and bottom of the computer screen, confusion and impatience are constant threats to a campaign seeking to have its message considered at length. The well-designed campaign Web site states its appeal clearly on the first page a visitor sees. But if the visitor goes no farther, then the experience is hardly more substantive than a yard sign. Indeed, as a tool of persuasion the Web site may be inferior. The yard sign can be situated precisely where the voters of a specific locality pass by it, including undecided voters and non-Net users as well as those leaners wont to head to a Web site. A passerby may even know the occupants of the building with the yard sign, in which case the sign communicates a personal endorsement.

As with television advertisements, the production values of political Web sites have suffered by comparison with commercial ones. Campaigners have been slow to learn how to translate their messages into the language of interactive graphics. The Web site of Russell Feingold's 1998 campaign to retain his Senate seat from Wisconsin was a laudable exception. It featured "The Fabulous Neumann Shell Game." The game consisted of a five-by-five matrix that displayed issue positions of opponent Mark Neumann regarding the federal budget and his Social Security reform proposal. Each box could be clicked on to see what enacting any two of Neumann's claims together would imply for the national balance sheet. Wherever the visitor clicked, "No! Budget Buster!" or "No! Doesn't Work!" would pop into view. The game engaged Web site visitors by putting them through a simulation of the very work officials must do while governing (but not campaigning): reconciling their positions in order to achieve fiscal responsibility.

Bob Drake, a candidate for Hamilton County (Ohio) treasurer in 2000, devised a more elaborate game on the same theme. "Stadium

Fiasco" staked players to $450 million in tax dollars and challenged them to build a football stadium according to the real-life Cincinnati counterpart's specifications. As the dollar counter dwindled, players clicked and dragged price-tagged pieces onto a grid ("Luxury Box," "Trees," "Parking," "Goal Posts"). The race against the disappearing public funds was vitiated by pop-up crisis alerts: "Uh-Oh—Cracks discovered in foundation. FIX THEM! Cost: $10 million"; "Install smoothie bar in players' lounge: $500,000." With "Stadium Fiasco," Web site visitors not only learned through a simulated government process but experienced a mock version of the public frustration the candidate wanted to drum up over the issue. The game ended with reprints of two newspaper articles and a traditional message from the candidate. (As of August 2003, it was still at www.bobdrake.org.)

Games are wonderful assets for a campaign Web site. They teach complex lessons by doing, and they have long proved their popularity with computer users. (Microsoft does not bundle "Minesweeper" and "FreeCell" into Windows without good reason.) Sometimes the great game of politics itself can provide a good opportunity to win publicity and support. The Iowa caucus may be the most complicated gauntlet voters go through in the presidential election system; its five stages require supporters to show up at meetings over a span of several months. In 2000, the Web sites of both the Bill Bradley campaign and the Iowa Republican Party featured step-by-step tutorials on how to participate. The Bradley site's tutorial logged in eight hundred people, which turned out to be 2 percent of the total Democratic turnout. This exemplifies the use of the Internet as a tool of persuasion—"Netoric," if you will—to warm the hearts of every political scientist: to win, your people must know the ropes; for a long shot to win, new people must be (brought in and) taught the ropes; through the Internet, new people can be taught the ropes on their own time, at their own pace . . . until the moment they must stand up and be counted.

For those moments of decision, the Web site will not do. It is too risky to presume that those impressed by their visit will return there when the campaign needs them. As information browsers and consumers, once people have examined a campaign Web site, they have little reason to return. Why look at the same material twice when there is so much to see elsewhere? A campaign that attempts to convince visitors to bookmark its Web site must establish itself, in effect, as a source of news, excitement, or some other frequently recurring good. That has turned out to be difficult for any political Web site, let alone one sponsored by a campaign. In 2000, only 7 percent of online seekers of election news—a subpopulation geared to the topic—went most often to candidate Web sites, as compared with 55 percent heading to national and local news organization sites and 27 percent relying on news sites at commercial portals such as AOL, MSN, and Yahoo. In 2002, with less news coverage devoted to elections for want of a presidential race, those heading most often to candidate Web sites jumped to 11 percent, but the overwhelming majority (64 percent) still preferred news organization sites, with news viewers at portals dropping to 19 percent.[2]

THE VIRTUES OF CAMPAIGN E-MAIL

There is a far better way to grab and hold Web site visitors in a campaign loop, and that is via e-mail. Where politics is concerned, a flimsy e-mail list will outperform a sterling Web site ninety-nine days out of one hundred. (The hundredth day, so to speak, occurs when a special event such as a televised debate attracts all sorts of attention to a campaign, attention that a smart campaign will funnel to its site.) E-mail is delivered; Web sites must be found. E-mail is easy to read; Web sites must be navigated. E-mail is easy to respond to; Web site responses engender frames within frames. Costs can be kept to a minimum since e-mail "production values" conventionally consist of a few lines of text. Distribution costs plummet toward zero for each additional address. Finally, e-mail is harder than a Web site for the press and opposition to monitor.

What do campaigns garner through e-mail? At a minimum, e-mail recipients may recognize the campaign name in the sender column of their mailbox and have its association reinforced with a campaign message in the subject column, even if they promptly delete the message without opening it. When e-mail recipients take the next step and open the message, they may be moved by what they see into making a commitment to the campaign: to accept further messages, to donate money, to forward messages to friends, to volunteer. These decisions carry them over the fence separating the spectators from the political players. They become extras who can respond to the call for a crowd scene.

When "extras" forward messages to others via e-mail, the activity infuses a campaign with the power of "word of mouse." Campaigns attempt, through "viral marketing" techniques, to simulate the sponta-neous phenomenon of spreading the word, asking e-mail recipients and Web site visitors to forward messages to friends. There is an advantage to the campaign in having that forwarding done through a form on the Web site because it can then keep close tabs on how broadly the message is being distributed. All the same, the key is to establish lines of communi-cation radiating out from a campaign, through its supporters, to other Net users who would never think of visiting a campaign Web site. Through e-mail, a campaign can summon specific supporters to take spe-cific actions at specific times much better than through a Web site.

E-mail has drawbacks, as competitors in the telemarketing and direct mail trades will eagerly point out. It is harder to ascertain the fate of an e-mail delivery than a letter, phone call, or for that matter, residential visit. E-mail lacks both a physical presence and a metaphysical suggestion of effort behind that presence, qualities that grassroots advocates count on to make an impression on a decisionmaker. Direct mail stacks up in the office; phone calls tie up office lines; visitors clog reception rooms—but e-mail may be deleted in a few seconds or even automatically. Moreover, unsolicited e-mail incites some of its recipients to resent or, still worse, retaliate against its senders.[3] Although "spam" may be no more irritating than the dinner-hour phone solicitation or the faux official letter that turns out to be a credit card come-on (certainly spam can be disposed of more quickly), campaigns must proceed gingerly in contacting people through the Internet without their permission. The main risk with unso-licited e-mail is that irate targets may protest to their Internet service provider (ISP), a private company, which may well respond by cutting off delivery service for the sender.

Still, for most online campaigners, e-mail's pluses have outweighed its minuses. During the 1990s, political professionals converged on the strat-egy of bringing people into a Web site, making a case for support, and asking them to deposit their e-mail address on their way out. Existing sup-porters could be asked for their e-mail addresses by other methods. As Republican National Committee chairman Jim Nicholson said, "Building our e-mail database is our 'job one' here."[4] By Election Day 2000, the GOP had collected close to one million e-mail addresses. That constituted the makings of a digital political machine, whereby grassroots support-ers could be alerted as quickly as flipping a switch. Because informa-tion is not tantamount to power, grassroots activation is never that simple, though. An e-mail recruitment and mobilization strategy places a cre-ative burden on the campaign to write seductive subject lines, so that recipients will want to open a message. "What Jay Leno Has to Say about Al Gore" was a big winner for the RNC in the fall of 2000.

Advocacy groups as well as candidate campaigns have embraced online publicity. Americans for Gun Safety, "a nonpartisan advocacy group designed to work on a retail franchise model," may owe its Net savvy to its founder, the head of the job-finding service Monster.com. In October 2000, television ads featuring John McCain referred viewers in Colorado and Oregon to the group's Web site. (The ads successfully urged passage of state ballot referenda proposing mandatory background checks at gun shows.) At the Web site, home page tabs led visitors to maps of the United States that indexed information, by state, on gun laws, gun fatalities, and local chapters of the organization. Along with procuring e-mail addresses to create a national database, then, Americans for Gun Safety sought to build state-by-state networks and local chapters. This federated approach, typical of advocacy groups in the early years of the twentieth century, is well served by the scalable quality of communication.[5] Effectively organized e-mail lists can be subdivided or amalgamated to suit any number of strategic moves.

Procuring e-mail addresses from the donors, newsletter subscribers, and other members of an advocacy organization can be a prologue to enhancing grassroots activities. It is one of several list-building methods that will become commonplace to the list manager, a key role to fill in the nascent digital political machine. List managers also will compile e-mail addresses using the same publicity techniques used to disseminate a campaign Web site address. They will stage contests, award prizes, and devise similar incentives to spur volunteers to collect the most e-mail members within a given time period. It is an open question whether they will swap, rent, and purchase lists—that is a common practice off-line, but online it flouts the spam taboo.

Building lists constitutes the first step. Lists must then be verified; Internet users, like singles in bars, have been known to give out false contact information to wooers. Next, the list manager will attempt to thicken the bonds between the campaign and its nominal supporters by forwarding items of interest, asking small favors, and heaping on the gratitude when the favors (campaign tasks) are granted. The ultimate test, of course, will occur on Election Day and its analogues in the policy-making processes of government. Some of the activity generated by list managers will be automated. Much of it will be tracked. And list managers might even come to implement suggestions offered, unprompted, from people on the list—something that finally happened, as noted in the

Preface, in 2003 during the Howard Dean campaign. All of these developments would be a manifestation of democratic action not requiring the "grassroots" modifier.

The virtues of e-mail were not lost on the 2000 Bush-Cheney campaign. Karl Rove, a direct mail specialist before graduating to general strategist, grasped e-mail's strengths and oversaw its use in the presidential campaign. According to Daron Shaw, the Bush campaign built its e-mail list up to 1.5 million names and used it "to publicize local events, disseminate information, respond to attacks, and coordinate Election Day activities."[6] The Gore campaign also used e-mail effectively, especially in battling the Bush campaign over the way a news story would play. Where Bush sought to win the daily competition in the media by disseminating Gore "exaggerations" through e-mail, Gore distributed e-mails with Bush "mistakes."[7]

These real-time, rhetorical e-mail battles reached an extreme on September 17, 2000. That day, the Bush and Gore campaigns for president besieged the reporters on their press e-mail lists (consisting of 2,000 and 1,200 names, respectively) with fifty-six e-mails. Most of these concerned a sixteen-page "Blueprint for the Middle Class" issued by the Republican nominee. The Democrat's "pre-buttal" (for it was released prior to the Bush document) was twenty-four pages long. The fifty-six e-mails spun, re-spun, and meta-spun (if that is a word adequate to describe commenting with intent to persuade on another's efforts at commenting with intent to persuade) around the topic of which candidate had the better economic plan for America.[8] At some point, this e-mail fusillade became counterproductive; the combatants had better things to do, and recipients tuned out. But with e-mail, the situation is more a function of audience tolerance than campaign resources.

THE DIGITAL ROAD DIARY

In 1998, the Jeb Bush for Governor campaign, working with Mike Connell of New Media Communications, developed a way to cultivate popular support among the electorate that integrated publicity with public appearances by the candidate. The sequence began with the campaign team and network drumming up local interest in the candidate's next event through e-mail and other channels of communication. When Bush showed up at the local school, plant, or mall, campaign workers gathered as many new names and e-mail addresses as possible. The follow-ups began with individual thank-yous, featuring, where possible, digital photos commemorating a handshake with the candidate. The follow-ups continued with invitations to join the campaign and, at the right time, reminders to get out and vote.

In small-budget campaigns, candidates can use e-mail in combination with their Web sites to be their own list managers, schedulers, and publicists. Andy Brack socked away a few hundred e-mail addresses when, in 1999, he hit the "meat and three [vegetables] for $5.99 circuit" in hopes of winning an open congressional seat from South Carolina in 2000. He sorted the contact information into lists by county and, for his out-of-state contributors, by metropolitan area. More imaginatively, as Brack walked and talked (and supped), he kept an campaign diary. He uploaded people's names and—thanks to a digital camera—faces into his narrative, right next to his mileage count and the route he would be taking in the coming days.

Brack usually found a way to weave politics into his cyber-journal, too:

CAMPAIGN DIARY (9/20/99): Helping in Stormy Weather
A Message from Andy Brack

Greetings to everyone. I hope the worst of Hurricane Floyd (traffic jams, rain, leaks, flooding and more) has passed you by. And I hope everything bodes well now.

Unfortunately, there's still more rain and bad weather particularly from flooding that's going to hit the northern part of the South Carolina coast. Myrtle Beach-area officials tell me that the Waccamaw River might not crest until next week. That means lots of extra water will fill the swamps. In recent years, as my friend Arthur Winston of Bucksport knows, people have been building in swamp areas Mother Nature might not have intended to be used for housing.

Regardless, there are ways the campaign can help coordinate help [sic]. If you live in the Conway area and need help or if you live somewhere else and want to help, send the campaign an e-note or give us a call and we'll do what we can.

Through entries like this, Brack made a multidimensional, down-home play for his candidacy. He recruited supporters, built team spirit, and established himself as a trustworthy, knowledgeable, and winsome fellow. He could not have done this without the Internet. Consider the alternatives: Brack would have had an impossible time persuading a media outlet to run his campaign diary on a one-day basis, let alone on a serial-and-perpetual basis (that is, with the latest and all previous installments available). Self-publication and distribution would not have been cheap; further, for a party or interest group to have done it would have negated the diary's individualist appeal. Moreover, in published form, no one could instantly respond to the road diary by contributing a name, address, comment, some dollars.

Brack did not come close to winning the congressional seat. He won 36 percent of the vote, just behind Gore's 38 percent in the district. However, the spending gap was narrower: Brack reported $486,323 in receipts, compared with $629,817 for his opponent, Henry Brown, Jr. Brown, a member of the dominant party in the state and district, had held office in the state legislature for fifteen years, including the previous six as chairman of the South Carolina House Ways and Means Committee. Brack chose not to challenge Brown in 2002. He did leave a marker, in the form of a parody site, abouthenrybrown.com, which satirizes the first-term member's votes and public statements. To the extent Brack maintains the site and, more important, his e-mail network, he could get back up to speed faster someday as a second-time candidate. And while he could not walk significantly faster, a diary would enable him to keep in touch with donors and voters—prospective, first-time, second-time, and so on—with an efficiency and style rarely seen before.

The digital road diary served as the precursor to the official campaign blog. The blog added the capability of outside comments and blog-to-blog links. Those touched by the candidate, and kept in touch with by the campaign, could now touch back—and outward to other people—all in the same software program, and all in the same folksy manner.

THE "FOREVER" PROBLEM

There is a catch to online publicity: while a campaign can take down whatever it puts up, any message someone has downloaded can be republicized by that person at any time. The ineradicability of Net postings enhances democracy. Manipulation, distortion, sensationalism, and other moral failings that persist in such "stealth media" as direct mail and telephone calls can be more readily traced to their perpetrators on the

Internet. But knowing that the slightest e-mail or Web page material lives forever, a few keystrokes away from the public square, does not make a campaign's publicity calculus any easier. For all that the Internet does to enhance the capacity to release a message and track its distribution, the new medium represents an overall decrease, not an increase, in what a campaign can presume to know with respect to what others know about it.

The new, Net-revamped economics of research and politics of publicity affected a tight 1998 race for a congressional seat in Connecticut. Jason Linde, the campaign manager for the incumbent Democrat Jim Maloney, discovered on the Web site of Republican challenger Mark Nielsen a transcript of his September 2, 1997, speech announcing his candidacy. In the speech, the Republican proposed cutting government at all levels so that the total tax take would not exceed 20 percent of national personal income. The speech had been delivered months before Linde accepted the post, and the Nielsen campaign was no longer emphasizing that point. Before long, however, the Democrats were attacking "Mark Nielsen's Extreme Plan," spelling out what it would mean for Social Security and Medicare benefits. The Nielsen campaign never really responded. Maloney retained his seat, and professional politicians had a cautionary tale to heed: campaigns are accountable for everything they release in the digital age.

To old-school politicians, the impossibility of taking posted messages out of circulation is so unbearable a risk as to make online publicity not worth the effort. But, as Dan Schnur of the McCain 2000 campaign points out, the same limitless space that enables detractors to bait someone as a "flip-flopper" or "hypocrite" also enables the target to get off the hook by providing ample context for controversial remarks. When McCain was accused of doing a special favor for a friend by writing a letter to the FCC, the McCain campaign responded by posting a slew of letters McCain had written on behalf of constituents, documenting that it was no special favor but ordinary activity for an elected representative.

There is an easy form of insurance campaigns can take out against Web-sprung charges. The protocol of time-stamping each posted item with the date of its original release contains the germ of a defense against antagonistic repostings and fake statements. A campaign that time-stamps its postings can credibly respond to a "Your views are poll-driven" or "You've covered up the truth" attack in several ways. It can stand by an authenticated string of consistent statements over a period of years. It can brandish an authentic original as evidence that the reposter has distorted the message. Or it can legitimately argue that a genuine shift of position reflects change in the world. In any case, time-stamping assures campaigns that engaging in publicity does not mean ceding all control over the life span and reproductions of its messages.

Time-stamping is standard procedure in news releases and official documents, and it is automatic in videotaping. Making it standard in campaign Web sites and e-mail would show the public how seriously a campaign is committed to its principles and to telling the truth, even while taking note of changing conditions. It recalibrates the balance of costs and benefits in favor of bringing a message as soon as possible.

Essentially, campaigns today must choose between framing their online image and being framed by others. Since every campaign is discussed, indexed, and archived online regardless of whether it sets up a Web site and e-mail operation, the right choice should be obvious. What campaigns resist, however, is not so much the logic of online publicity as the effort it requires. The "forever" problem means that someone associated with the digital political machine must be the content manager, coordinating the release of campaign material on the Internet and monitoring its fate as well as what else is said about the campaign online. Each online message will generate a pattern of dissemination from which lessons must be drawn, enabling the content manager to weigh in on the basic decisions of strategic political communication: whether the campaign should go public and, if so, in whose name, when, in what forms, through which channels.

In 2002, Congressman Maloney of Connecticut (and campaign manager Linde) faced another incumbent, Republican Nancy Johnson, in a redrawn district. Early in October, the Johnson campaign posted a chart on its Web site home page comparing the number of bills sponsored by each incumbent that had been signed into law since 1997, when Maloney joined Johnson in Congress. The tally, also featured in Johnson television ads, was 23:1 in her favor. The Democrat responded with a similar chart on his home page, which put the count at 2:9 in his favor.

This was a substantive dispute over who was the more effective legislator. It challenged journalists and constituents to check the records. Although bill sponsorships and enactments would seem to be objective criteria, the complexity of the legislative process lent credence to both counts. (Bills get folded into other bills before final passage.) A good journalist and smart voter would find no simple answer to the basic question of effectiveness. But a Web search would enlighten them nevertheless. The exchange thus stands as a model of the kind of high-quality political content the Internet can host when campaigns take on the "forever" problem in a serious manner.

That list and content management are ideas whose time has not yet quite arrived can be inferred from the evidence of how campaigns deployed Web sites in the 2000 and 2002 cycles.[9]

CAMPAIGN WEB SITES: HIGHLIGHTS AND PATTERNS

There may be a nexus between good campaign Web sites and electoral victory, but one would be hard-pressed to discern it from the pattern of campaign Web sites to date. Internet Campaign Solutions (www. e-campaignsolutions.com), a consulting company that specializes in building Web sites for political organizations and campaigns, mounted an extensive content analysis of 2000 congressional campaign Web sites. It found no correlation between high Web site quality and victory—or, for that matter, between Web site sophistication and incumbency, party, or being from a high-tech jurisdiction. That said, a few results provided a glimmer of hope for those concerned about the impact of big money on elections: in six of the eight races rated a toss-up for the House and Senate in which a challenger unseated an incumbent in 2000, that challenger had what was deemed a better Web site, and five of the six spent less money on their campaigns than their opponents.[10]

In these early days of Net politics, the best predictor of Web site quality may simply be the presence of someone on the campaign team who cares about it. Such was the sensible hypothesis of Steven Schneider, a political scientist who directed the University of Pennsylvania's Net Election team (www.netelection.org, now defunct) in 2000 and, with Kirsten Foot, constructed the campaign Web site database www.politicalweb.info in 2002. Net Election and Political Web analyzed the Web sites of candidates for Congress and governor, and while the universes of sites analyzed differ slightly, the numbers are comparable. At a January 10, 2001, news conference releasing the Net Election data, panelist Jeff Stanger provided the most incisive analysis of why certain Web site features appeared in the patterns they did. He was uniquely positioned to do so: Stanger, an alumnus of the Annenberg Public Policy Center, which houses the team, opened his own political Web site company for the 2000 cycle, www.netcampaign. com. The site he built for Jean Elliott Brown, a candidate for Congress in Florida, was highly regarded within the Net politics community.

Stanger classified each Web site feature by two criteria: whether it was easy or hard to do and whether it benefited mostly the campaigner or the voter. By "hard to do" he meant a feature that would require considerable content development time and programming sophistication. No surprise: the easy features were found more frequently than the hard ones. Slight surprise: of the easy set, two voter-serving features topped the chart—candidate biographies (present on 89 percent of the 2000 cycle's campaign Web sites and 88 percent in 2002) and issue position statements (75 percent and 83 percent, respectively). Of course, while biographies help voters, they also flatter candidates.

Next in popularity on the easy side of the ledger came a trio of candidate-serving attributes: volunteer sign-up pages (68 percent; 62 percent), contribution forms (60 percent; 55 percent), and press releases (52 percent; 2002 data unavailable). At the bottom of the easy-to-do list were mentions of the opponent on the front page (16 percent; 2002 data unavailable) and a link to the opponent's site (1 percent; 1 percent). The latter took courtesy to the point of absurdity: why help a visitor leave your site for the opposition's? Only academics could expect to find such a feature helpful. The former was a missed opportunity to sharpen advantageous contrasts between the candidates in voters' minds.

To some extent, candidates drew favorable contrasts and attacked their opponents outright on satellite Web sites linked to the virtual campaign headquarters. Lynn Reed pioneered this technique in a 1998 congressional race. Her attack site www.missedvotes.com led with a quote of Republican nominee Don Benton that he did not "miss any of the important votes" while serving in the Washington state legislature. Visitors were invited to judge for themselves; the site featured a drop-down menu with "Missed Votes: Greatest Hits" and missed votes organized by year and subject area. Each page of missed votes linked to Democrat Brian Baird's main Web site. Isolating the attack page preserved the candidate's home site as a place with positive information and helped turn the satellite site into news story material (it being easier to peg a story to a new Web site than to a new page or section of an existing site), making a splash in the local media. The Baird campaign ran television spots pointing people to missedvotes.com, and the candidate cited it in his debates with Benton. The innovation contributed to Baird's victory.

Stanger placed only one Web site feature in the hard-to-do and candidate-benefiting category: a sign-up for the campaign e-mail list, which 44 percent of the 2000 class included (dropping to 35 percent in 2002). This confirms the growing awareness of what can be done with lists; it is worth the maintenance time required. In the last quadrant, hard to do and voter benefiting, the pertinent features were unsurprisingly adopted by only a few campaigns. Only 13 percent of 2000 campaign Web sites posted speeches (9 percent in 2002), and 6 percent sported television advertisements (2002 data unavailable). The low percentages illustrate just how early we are in the multimedia (or "convergence" or "broadband") phase of the Internet's public life. As video streaming becomes easier and less expensive (a possibility, not a certainty) for people to see and more campaigns come to terms with the "forever" problem, these figures may well rise.

The following features seem likely to remain rare, because they are frankly too idealistic for most politicians: explicit comparisons on the issues (12 percent in 2000, sinking to 4 percent in 2002), moderated discussion forums (3 percent; 2002 data unavailable), and identification of contributors (3 percent; 1 percent). Comparisons and, more to the point, contrasts on the issues can be fabulously enlightening, as the Feingold and Drake examples showed. But they go against the strategic convention that a campaign Web site ought to present only positive information. The online public likes comparisons, though. Researching engenders comparison making, and finding a ready-made comparison simplifies the activity. Nonetheless, voters are more likely to find candidate issue position comparisons on civic information sites such as Dnet.org and vote-smart.org and, to a narrower and sharper degree, on the sites of issue advocacy groups, political parties, and ad hoc coalitions. As for discussion forums, it may be that they are rare because no one has figured out a way to guarantee publicity from them; either they veer out of the campaign's control or sink into sententiousness. The pros and cons of identifying contributors are discussed in the next chapter.

The campaign Web site has been discussed excessively in proportion to its political utility, because of the splash the Web and Web browser made when they burst on the scene and because a Web site lends itself to analysis by outsiders. There is only so much a campaign can do when it has to wait for people to show up. But a Web site is undeniably valuable to campaigners as a means of acquiring e-mail addresses. Among major-party candidates for Congress and governorships, 46 percent had campaign Web sites in 1998, 68 percent did in 2000, and 76 percent in 2002.

The campaign Web site also is valuable to citizens and thus to democratic idealists. Campaigns can bring all their resources in every type of media to make a detailed case on a Web site, and this adds to the information voters can sort through at their own pace. A Web site can help connect voters to campaigns as well, to the extent the campaign posts calls to public meetings with the candidate and hosts those meetings on the Web site. This improves citizen access to political decisionmakers, especially for those who find it difficult to attend meetings, such as workaholics, the disabled, and the weather-bound. That campaigns are likely to do these things in a selective, biased, and sporadic fashion by no means diminishes their value to democracy, so long as nonpartisan information and routes connecting citizens with each other are available elsewhere on the Web.

4

ONLINE ADVERTISING AND FUND-RAISING: WHERE IS THE MONEY?

Advertising and fund-raising are the primary arteries and veins for campaign money. They also are the most controversial aspects of professional campaigning today. As the Internet emerged, civic activists turned off by the excesses and disparities of the money-politics nexus looked to cyberspace as a place where, as the catchphrase put it, the playing field could be leveled and candidates could demonstrate their superiority on the basis of their arguments and records instead of their televised images and bank accounts. Many political professionals, by contrast, saw the Internet as a field where millions of dollars could be honorably extracted and expended in the service of campaigns they supported.

The Bipartisan Campaign Reform Act (often called McCain-Feingold or Shays-Meehan after its congressional sponsors) became law in 2002 and went into effect the day after the 2002 general elections. However, speculation about the act's passage, contents, and impact created background noise to efforts at online fund-raising and advertising in the 2000 and 2002 election cycles. The particulars of the bill that was passed revolved around the regulation of certain categories of advertising and fund-raising, and the Internet was a tangential consideration. It was the debate that arose over campaign finance reform legislation that really had provided a forum for the perennial dispute over what money can buy in American politics, and the Internet played a role in this larger discussion. What the bill couldn't fix, perhaps the new technology could.

ONLINE ADVERTISING STALLS

The pioneers of online advertising and fund-raising gathered steam and venture capital from an incentive their counterparts in research, publicity, and mobilization lacked: ad makers and ad placers, and to a lesser extent fund-raisers, are traditionally paid on commission, not simply by fee or salary. In the world at large, one election cycle with a big-time client at the 15 percent standard rate can turn a media consultant into a millionaire. But as 2002 ended, the dot-pols had failed to develop reliable ways of making money for themselves in the course of spending and raising it for their clients. In retrospect, their failures are quite explainable in terms of unresolved procedural complications, problems that may or may not be solved in the coming years. Yet these complications hit the dot-pols largely by surprise. At first glance in the late 1990s, online advertising and fund-raising looked like surefire, even "turnkey," applications of the new communications technology.

In the winter of 1999–2000, the final four presidential candidates— Bill Bradley, George W. Bush, Al Gore, and John McCain—purchased online advertisements prior to the Iowa caucus and New Hampshire primary. The novelty and competitive context of these buys garnered them news coverage.[1] That should have started a cycle of advertising and news about online advertising. News stories in which advertising can be described as powerful or fascinating are popular with media corporations, because such stories implicitly showcase the media themselves as good places for marketers to spend money. Indeed, the very word "media" originated in connection with advertising: a medium is a communication channel that carries ads.[2] So as these four high-profile politicians began online advertising, there was already a financial incentive for the media to commission and disseminate features about those ads, profiles of their makers, analyses of their contents, and speculations about their impact on the race for the presidency. In turn, further news stories about online ads would have motivated the campaigns to develop more ads, the better to win still more "free media" coverage. Campaigners would have been motivated for strategic reasons to create online ads, talk them up, and watch the hot ones dart around and around the interior wall separating the news and advertising divisions of multimedia corporations.

This cycle did not materialize, though. In the fall of 2000, the Democratic National Committee purchased only one banner advertisement, while the Republican National Committee was slightly more ambitious.[3] Reports of candidates, parties, and issue advocacy groups placing online ads were virtually nonexistent. This may have been because such arrangements were few and far between, but even the ads that were bought garnered little attention; a multistate, last-minute $100,000 buy by the Gore campaign received no coverage. An industry representative, speaking at a postelection conference of dot-pols, with every reason to put the best statistics forward, estimated that in the 2000 election campaigners allotted 0.1 percent of their budgets to online ads.[4]

Comparison with the early years of television casts this stalling of online advertising in a bleak light. In 1952, the second presidential campaign in which commercial television was available, spots for Dwight Eisenhower (and to a lesser extent Adlai Stevenson) attracted much public discussion. Eisenhower's Madison Avenue consultant, Rosser Reeves, of the agency BBD&O, won renown that year as a campaign mastermind. But in 2000, when a higher percentage of Americans had Web access than had television in 1952, no online firm, consultant, or advertisement did likewise. This despite the concerted effort by a few figures to stir up such attention.

Was the hype and hope for online advertising premature? Or was and is there something intrinsic to the Internet that stymies effective advertising?

THE CASE FOR ONLINE POLITICAL ADVERTISING

By 1999, vendors and brokers of online ads had loaded their sales pitches with a host of good reasons why campaigns should spend money on them.[5] Their PowerPoint presentations revolved around seven propositions:

- *Online advertising efficiently publicizes campaign Web sites.* If there is going to be a campaign Web site, the candidate ought to advertise it online. Web sites depend on ancillary publicity for traffic, and online ads can bring strangers into a Web site with one click. That click can be tracked by origin, time of entry and exit, and other criteria; the "click-through" is a basic unit of online advertising analysis and pricing.

- *Online advertising is a cost-effective medium to get out a message.* Considered in terms of cost per thousand (or "CPM," with the M standing for the Roman numeral), the Net delivers more "page views" or viewer "impressions" for less money than either direct (surface) mail or telemarketing, to say nothing about the mass media, which do not elicit direct responses.[6] This is especially true for text ads, with their tiny production costs. But it also is true of multimedia ("rich media") ads.

- *Viewers of online ads can be moved into action at once.* Not only do online ads lead to direct responses, they do so immediately. Joining an e-mail list, the most fundamental of responses, is a mark of a "conversion," another unit of analysis and pricing. A conversion of an ad viewer into a name on a sponsor list indicates that an ad has succeeded. The corresponding "CPA," or cost per acquisition, of online advertising is lower than for direct mail and telemarketing.

- *The Internet offers advertisers the opportunity to microtarget,* that is, to aim messages at viewers with even greater precision than is possible in the notably segmented media of cable television, radio, surface mail, magazines, and zoned newspapers. Like the segmented media, the Internet permits ads to be directed at people who belong to specific demographic and geographic categories. But online ads can be further subdivided on the basis of initial responses. For example, an online ad can be sent to those sports fans in Georgia ages seventeen to thirty-five who responded to a previous ad (or, controversially, who responded to an online ad from someone else whose data the advertiser has obtained).

- *Online ads can be customized for different audiences, simultaneously and serially.* The low production costs, negligible distribution costs, and ease of targeting of online ads enable campaigns to vary and fine-tune their appeals on the fly. For example, in 2000 the Republican National Committee rotated an ad that read, "The future President wants to see you . . . " with one that read, "We want you to WIN a Palm Digital Assistant." Both teasers required viewers to enter an e-mail address before permitting them to see the remainder of the ad, thereby combining the click-through and conversion stages and predicating both on the viewer's curiosity instead of a rational choice to get involved.

Hypothetically, this example could be taken further. Those responding to the first ad could have been slated to see a second ad, "The future President is coming to your state. . . . " when appropriate;

the rest of the ad, with a sign-up box to attend a function with the nominee, would be visible only to those making a pledge. Meanwhile, those responding to the second ad could have been enticed to enter another raffle for a high-tech product. In such fashion, online ads could operate as quasi-retail campaigns within wholesale campaigns, acting to simulate a conversation, if not a sustained relationship, between a customer and salesperson. (This pseudo-intimacy was satirized in the 2002 sci-fi movie *Minority Report,* in which ads emanating from hidden speakers whispered the hero's name as he ran through a shopping mall, enticing him into various stores.)

- *Online ads can be measured and evaluated with incomparable accuracy and speed.* The online advertiser can within hours review data reports with click-through and conversion rates across microtargeting categories and with respect to different versions of an appeal. Supplied with such feedback, the campaign can optimize the efficiency and effectiveness of its advertising content, distribution, and timing—in print and broadcast and mail and phone and in person, as well as through online media.

- *Online ads lend themselves to surprise tactics.* An online ad can never be as opaque to the press, the opposition, or the regulators as its telephone or direct mail counterparts. As discussed in Chapter 3, it only takes one Net recipient to forward a message and raise its public profile. Therefore, the Internet is not a great "stealth" medium. But it is not bad. Absent a tip or leak, would-be monitors of online advertising face billions of Web pages to search. A skilled research professional can cut down the task considerably; all the same, campaigns can catch others off guard. As noted previously, the Gore campaign managed to advertise in eleven states on Yahoo! and AOL three days before the election without media notice.[7] Had the Bush campaign caught wind of this, it could have countered.

The sales presentations did not mention another reason for political operatives to start buying online ads, but it is worth stating the obvious here: advertising is a highly regarded tool in campaign politics, as it is in most aspects of American life. Advertising attracts so much media attention that a person could be forgiven for equating it with publicity, even though the latter term embraces direct sales, the staging of events, and the courting of the press along with commercials. With the advertising mentality so pervasive in society, migration to the new medium by campaign professionals should have been a no-brainer. Indeed, the flexibility of online ads should have held special appeal to political clients, whose campaigns tend to be shorter, more intense, and subject to more changes in environment than those of commercial clients. But the candidates took a pass in 2000, and in 2002 as well.

The Problems with Online Advertising

What accounted for the paucity of online ads? The dot-pols I have interviewed and listened to in forums cited several obstacles and objections they encountered as they tried to sell the concept of online ads to political candidates, organizations, and advocates. First, the bursting of the high-tech stock bubble had ramifications for online advertising. The advertising community is by its nature sensitive to social trends. That helps explain why, as online ad rates sank from $42 CPM to $8 and lower in 2000, demand did not rise as the basic law of the market would predict.

A second problem concerned the limited reach of the Internet. Some political clients, especially Democrats, believed the comparative advantages of online advertising would not work in their favor until a greater percentage of the voting populace regularly used the new medium. As political analyst Hugh Carter Donahue has noted, John Street won the Philadelphia mayoralty in 1999 with the help of a publicity technology suited to his electoral base: a Polaroid camera.[8] Street's supporters were far more likely to be reached—and impressed—by being handed a snapshot of the candidate posing with them than by a banner advertisement. Andrew Brack of South Carolina, as knowledgeable about and committed to online politics as anyone who could be found among candidates for Congress in 2000, advertised on the home page of the Myrtle Beach newspaper's Web site. He estimated that one hundred thousand people a month saw his ad, and a thousand clicked through to his Web site—but television, radio, and personal appearances garnered him far more attention and, for that matter, e-mail addresses.[9]

Voter Files, Privacy, and Spam

Third, campaigns would dive into online advertising at the risk of antagonizing public opinion on the rising policy issue of individual privacy and the less intense but broader irritation at receiving unsolicited e-mails, or "spam." Online privacy activists were well organized, and their opinions carried extra weight because they were, in many cases, Internet pioneers. They warned ordinary users to be suspicious of how ads happened to appear before them and to be careful about volunteering information about themselves. Lauren Weinstein of the online newsletter *Privacy Forum Digest* wrote after the presidential ad buys of December 1999:

> The power of Web data collection, tracking, ad presentation, and similar technologies, combined with other traditionally public record data sources (and voter registration roles are just the tip of the iceberg), creates a scenario that might cause Darth Vader to be jealous.[10]

Controversies involving firms that collect data about individuals signaled the potency of the privacy issue as a deterrent to online advertising (and other Net activities). In March 2000, the online profiling firm DoubleClick canceled plans to merge with Abacus Direct, which owned data culled from mail-order and retail chain purchases. In the same time period, AOL and Microsoft each pulled out of deals with Aristotle Industries, which maintains the nation's biggest compendium of information about voters, larger than those of either major political party. These actions were hugely important, because voter files, as compiled by the election departments of governments and souped up into databases by entrepreneurs like Aristotle, are precious currency to political professionals.

Despite the name, voter files do not contain information on how individuals have voted. (The privacy of the act of voting is in greater danger of being compromised by online voting than by the dot-pols.) Voter files contain records of an individual's party registration and attendance record, so to speak, on election days. They may be the best single predictor available of voting performance. In 2000, nearly half the Senate and House members, and state political parties were Aristotle clients. The meshing of Aristotle's voter files with other databases might well have made microtargeted online advertising irresistible; AOL or Microsoft could have offered political clients access to those sports fans in Georgia ages seventeen to thirty-five who responded to a previous ad from them *and* were likely Republican voters. But neither of the ISP giants agreed to provide Aristotle with access to their databases of e-mail and billing addresses.[11] The public reaction would have been riotous; in some states, furthermore, the commercial use of voter file information is illegal.

Consequently, when a campaign in 2000 asked a dot-pol pitching online advertising whether ads could be targeted to registered Democrats who voted in the last election, the dot-pol had to answer no. By 2002, other microtargeting techniques were emerging that claimed to reach likely voters at a better rate than voter files. Essentially, they matched targeting information with likely online haunts (for example, to reach the above category without the party identification in close approximation, place an ad on www.nascar.com). But that was a tough sell in a milieu addicted to voter file data. The taboo on merging voter files with online information identifying individuals is likely to stay in place.

In pulling out of the Aristotle deals, the ISPs may have considered public opinion as well as the resistance of privacy activists and the limits of the law. The annual UCLA Internet survey found in 2000 that 64 percent of Net users agreed or strongly agreed that they put their privacy at risk while online.[12] Spam was a popular concern. A Democracy Online Project survey in 2001 found that 54 percent of Net users were bothered by unsolicited political e-mail.[13] Anxiety about privacy was not necessarily the reason. Junk e-mail is disliked on its own terms, even when it does not arrive on the basis of microtargeted information.

It is not known how widespread or intense the general loathing of aggressive Internet commercialization is or will remain. Ads may have a way of breaking down consumer resistance through cleverness and repetition. They may become less objectionable online once the demarcation lines separating paid from editorial content are clarified. Still, the backlash could strangle online advertising, especially in the political sphere, where oppositional struggle and news coverage are always poised to amplify the actions of a few. No candidate wants to be called a spammer in a debate.

A CHAOTIC PROCESS

The fourth and perhaps the main obstacle to the growth of online advertising was bound up in the disarray attending the process of deciding on an online ad strategy, implementing it, and gauging the results. Advertising is inherently complicated because at least four different parties are involved: the client, the ad maker, the time or space buyer, and the media outlets. Bureaucratization reduces the complexity of this four-sided transaction. When political managers want to advertise their candidate, cause, or coalition through the mass media, they can rely on a set of well-defined roles, routines, and rules of thumb. They have a good idea of how many times a commercial needs to air, or a print ad needs to run, so it may be considered "seen" by a targeted population. They can obtain rate cards from the stations and publications in their market, so they know how much it will cost to reach the desired saturation level with their ad. They know how far in advance to contact the media outlet. And so on. Similar routines, greased by well-accepted benchmarks, help campaigns allocate funds for telemarketing, direct mail, and neighborhood canvassing, the customary channels by which donors and volunteers are acquired.

Online, in contrast, the absence of roles, routines, and rules was aggravated by a plurality of goals and a profusion of options. In the world beyond the computer screen, mass media ads are conventionally used to brand a name and message upon a target population's mind, while direct response media are used to raise money and harness volunteers. Online, campaigns can deploy ads to do either or both, or neither. Perhaps identity branding and network building are less important than brandishing power, that is, making the press, the opposition, the high-tech elites, and opinion leaders aware that the campaign "gets" the Internet and is a serious player in a political contest. In that case, a third ad strategy mixing highly specialized buys with such staples of Washington publicity life as the news conference, editorial board meeting, and power lunch would be in order. The online components of such a strategy were untested.

Suppose, though, that someone was willing to take a stab at pursuing one or more of the three goals associated with advertising stated above. For instance, little-known candidates with lots of money often adopt a branding strategy, particularly in the early stages of a campaign. Proponents of online advertising could make a legitimate plea for some of the branding budget on the strength of the bullet points listed earlier. They could fortify their case by citing the Internet's growing population, its trendiness, and, above all, the fact that people log on while at work. A Rutgers University study released in February 2000 documented what many dot-pols sensed: half of the U.S. workforce spent at least an hour a day online, and 14 percent spent as much as half their day in front of a networked computer screen.[14] No other advertising medium could match that penetration into the workplace.

But the disarray would resurface in considering the ensuing braid of options. "Very well," a campaign client might say, "let's advertise online.

Which forms do you recommend?" The account-seeking team would have to start by running through the variety of advertising forms, aware that the client might not recognize the type even after the label was explained. *Banners* are rectangular boxes that stretch across a Web page; *skyscrapers* are banners rotated ninety degrees; there are other designated sizes and screen positions for Web page ads. *Interstitials,* also known as *pop-ups,* obscure part of the nonadvertising content of a Web page, forcing users to click either to get rid of them or to visit the sponsor's Web site. *Rich media* versions of online ads have animation features to draw the eye. *Link advertisements* result from an agreement between two entities to establish hyperlinks between (well-trafficked or frequently selected pages of) their sites. In *registration advertisements,* a client purchases a slot high on or next to a search engine list that is delivered in response to requests using specified key words. ("I want my candidate's campaign name, two-line description, and hyperlink displayed on the top of the page returned whenever someone is searching for information about high taxes.") *Co-registration ads* appear as Internet users fill out forms for another service or product. *Co-branded content* appears on informational pages about another service or product.

The choice of placement encompassed an even larger menu of options than the choice of forms. There were no reliable and systematically updated data on overall traffic to various Web sites carrying ads, let alone traffic targeted by groups or microtargeted by responses.[15] Assume, however, that the client could be handed a list of five online outlets that logically, if not verifiably, met the client's needs, such as www.nascar.com, or www.accessatlanta.com, to take a couple of examples. Our hopeful dot-pol would have to hesitate again, because of the tumultuous conditions in online advertising. One promising broker of online ads might go out of business before a buy could be completed. Another might offer a better deal than its more prominent competitor. A third might be merging with a larger firm with its own advertising representatives, protocols, and prices.

Pressing onward nevertheless, the next step would be to develop appropriate content for each ad form and projected placement. A family of ads, variations on one message, would be selected and placed. Then, when the first feedback data on an ad buy arrived, the ad team would confront its last set of options. For there was no standard formula to gauge results and guide optimization. How many exposures to an online ad would "move the meter" of name identification, say, ten percentage points in the campaign's polling?[16] Log files abounded with possibly relevant and significant metrics: page views, unique visitors, average time spent on a page, click-throughs, conversions, and so forth. The numbers might all point in the same direction, but that would signify nothing unless the advertisers, like social scientists, had set up adequate controls such that it was only the online advertising that was being assessed. Otherwise, the impressive spike in traffic might be attributable to the candidate's appearance in a public forum instead of the ad buy begun two days earlier.

The chaotic process meant that online advertising teams could not calculate their own costs, craft a plan, and set a price that could sustain and reward their efforts. That, in turn, meant that campaigns could not allocate a percentage of their budgets to online advertising with a reasonable expectation of what it would purchase. What seemed so promising in the abstract foundered on specifics. Thus, the murkiness of the process joined the discouraging business environment, the incomplete reach of the medium, and the problems of privacy and spam as concerns working against online advertising. The bottom line: while online advertising firms had plenty of general points to make to campaign clients, the best possible talking point—a bigger bang for the buck—was hard to make concrete.

All of which raises a larger question: will these obstacles be smoothed over sufficiently to make online advertising worthwhile in 2004, or anytime soon?

THE CASE AGAINST ONLINE ADVERTISING

The case against online advertising begins with the idea that—the terms "surf" and "browse" notwithstanding—people go online for specific reasons. Whether their objective is knowledge, social contact, news, games, or shopping, they will regard ads as objectionable interruptions. The word that matters is "objectionable." Ads are intrusions in almost every setting, but they do not always disturb. Many ads are designed and deployed on the assumption that people will not pay direct or serious attention to them.[17] Programs on television, the tail to the advertising dog, are typically innocuous in order to create a pleasant environment conducive to the subconscious reception of commercials. But online content cannot be as thoroughly controlled as television programs. Even if oligopoly comes to constrict the range of Web choices, Net users will regulate much of the flow and direction of information in accordance with their purposes. Online ads, then, may be destined to irritate because Net surfers and browsers are actually visitors and searchers. They are always headed for or engaged in a communicative task, and thus too mentally alert to accept ads without objection. No matter what an ad says or when and where it appears, an online recipient will regard it as a disturbance. Ads may yet be effective online, but their makers and vendors will not be able to claim a comparative media advantage.

The capacity for documenting every facet of online activity also may work against advertising in the new medium. The "granularity" and "transparency" of online communication might rob advertising of its allure, its power to insinuate desires only the product can satisfy. Audiences usually are presumed to be susceptible to commercials, yet this very presumption may be the industry's biggest sell. No one knows exactly how often magazines and mail go unopened, television programming gets zapped, newspapers are skimmed, and radio stations are switched. No one associated with mass media advertising even dares to suggest how many members of their target audiences take the desired action of purchasing the product or voting for the candidate. These vagaries allow the fantasy of persuasion by advertisement to be sustained by clients.

The feedback the Net makes available throws open the velvet curtain to reveal the limits of advertising. The detailed results of an online ad campaign are more likely to disappoint than thrill: only this many click-throughs, that many conversions. Worse, the results may spark questions about the effectiveness of the older media. The most vehement version of the case argues that the Net heralds the end of *all* advertising as an effective marketing tool. Seth Godin, a proponent of online retail marketing, contends that "our brains have shut down" from the explosion in exposure to advertisements and that "permission [to communicate with a customer or supporter] is the asset of the future." If contact is not anticipated, personal, and relevant, Godin says, it will be ignored. Such retailing cannot be done through display graphics, radio, television, newspapers, or periodicals.[18] These mass media will wither because both audiences and clients will come to prefer online retailing to any kind of broad-scale appeal.

Godin may or may not turn out to be prophetic. What is distinctive today about the Internet is the breadth of the space it occupies on the mass advertising–interpersonal marketing continuum. To say ads do not work online is not to condemn the Internet's potential as a marketplace. Big mass market advertisers such as Coca-Cola and Procter & Gamble are not buying many online ads; instead, they are luring people to their Web sites with promotional deals, harvesting e-mail addresses, and then alerting customers to new products accordingly. Which is to say, these companies have, at least as part of their strategy, disintermediated the advertising agency and Internet portal site from the sales process and have focused on creating new publicity pathways.[19] That paring away of two of the four parties to the advertising transaction does not bode well for the industry.

THE ONLINE ADVERTISING OUTLOOK

Online political advertising may not be the rocket to wealth and fame that it was for those who did television spots for presidential candidates. Online media companies may not survive, let alone thrive, on ad revenues alone. But online ads in commercial zones of the Web already make sense as part of a political strategy, if for no other reason than how inexpensive they are. More people may object to ads online than in any other medium, but evidence shows that they are remembered.[20] In its regular pitch in 2001, Mindshare Internet Campaigns claimed, on the basis of 125 million ad impressions it placed in 2000 for such advocacy clients as the Business Software Alliance, Citizens for Better Medicare, and People for the American Way, that it could recruit supporters to campaigns for half the cost of direct mail, in two days instead of three weeks.

One of Mindshare's approaches, according to its cofounder Jonah Seiger, involves starting with a target number of activists, calculating how many ad exposures it would take to engage them, and then, as a campaign begins, continually tweaking the advertising content and placement based on feedback data and early results.[21] Such a strategy, couched in small but specific expectations, with a margin for disappointing developments and a presumption that advertising is but one component of an online campaign, can acclimate a client to fluctuations in the returns. When a client complains, "Hey, I paid expecting a click-through rate of 1.5 percent, and last week it was down to 0.45 percent," the consultant can respond, "We set out to enlist people to help with the campaign, and here is what they have done so far." A fee-and-bonus pricing system suits this constant adjustment approach better than commissions.

It seems likely that existing obstacles, political and more general, to online advertising will either erode or be beaten down by bureaucratic procedure. Standards will be imposed on the online ad buying process:

independent sources will publish data metrics from which rules of thumb can be derived; a code of ethics will serve as a prophylactic against recurrent industry criticisms; and perhaps government regulations and laws will be passed to deal with outsize scandals. DoubleClick has recently announced software to help place advertisements in targeted e-mails.[22]

Some will groan at the growth of online advertising, seeing it as yet another victory for the crass over the artful, for consumerism over civics. (One industry representative says four words or their equivalents are the essential ingredients of every effective ad: Free! New! Sex! Unique!) These groaners will be in the minority—and they will constitute the market for ad-blocking software. In politics, the groaners will wax eloquent (or otherwise) in the news divisions of media companies as presidential candidates embrace the maturing industry sector. Those sounds will drive more traffic to view the online ads being referenced.

Online, as elsewhere, negative ads and ads that popular culture can embrace will draw attention. The highlights of the 2002 campaign, from an online politics watcher's vantage point, were attack sites and animated videos that sparked enough controversy to grab news coverage. Bill Simon and Tim Hagan, gubernatorial challengers in California and Ohio, respectively, won a media following and site traffic by riffing off corporate advertising campaigns. AFLAC sought a restraining order against Hagan's attack site www.Taftquack.com, which featured a quacking duck spoofing Governor Robert Taft. An Ohio lower court ruled that Taftquack qualified as protected political speech. Simon's campaign let it be known that eBay was concerned about its attack site, www.e-gray.org, which mimicked the auction pages of the Web giant to lance Gray Davis as a governor who sold out to special interests. In Georgia, a ten-minute epic depicting Governor Roy Barnes as a giant rat terrorizing the state helped Sonny Perdue, a little-known state senator, defeat two primary rivals and, in the fall's biggest upset, the incumbent.

At the national level, the standout example of a humorous online publicity stunt was a flash animation video entitled "Social Insecurity." Shipped the night of October 2 to Democratic National Committee e-mail subscribers and posted on the party Web site hours later, this online cartoon found an edgy way to make the point that privatization would have sent Social Security retirement accounts tumbling: a caricatured President Bush pushed an elderly woman in a wheelchair down a graph line symbolizing stock market declines of the past few years. The look and sound of the cartoon was vintage Road Runner. Its argument was almost as old, considering that in 1964 a Lyndon Johnson ad featured a pair of scissors snipping a Social Security card in half as a portent of what Barry Goldwater would do as president. The video mischief succeeded mainly because it got its target to cry foul. Republican National Committee chair Mark Racicot called the cartoon "beyond offensive." Perhaps it was—but when someone complains like that, who among us does not want to see what caused the stir?

The news media ate up the controversy. Matt Drudge linked to the video under the headline "Dems Depict Bush Murdering Senior." Over the next two days, half a million people visited the DNC Web site to rubberneck, as it were. The traffic might have been higher had the Internet as a whole and the DNC site in particular not suffered technical difficulties. It might have been much lower had the RNC issued no comment. The traffic spike and buzz around the capital lasted a week. For a brief time, the election was about Social Security, not just the war on terrorism. The RNC tried to fight fire with fire, posting a cartoon with Bush as Superman flying to the rescue of the elderly woman. Whereupon the DNC released a sequel it had commissioned, in which the woman arises from her crash to chide Bush about prescription drugs.

But the RNC had the last laugh. Members of its e-mail list, estimated at five million, received a "personalized interactive greeting card" on Election Day 2002, addressed from RNC deputy chairman Jack Oliver. To the strains of "Yankee Doodle Dandy," the video asked Net viewers to mark a mock ballot Republican or Democrat and then showed a happy or sad ending accordingly.

These humorous missives were publicity moves, not ads; they did not run on selected Web sites in exchange for money. But online ads that try to attract attention through lampooning and silliness seem the logical next step. People hard at work or study are often receptive to a break, and if they break by going online and encounter something that makes them laugh, the message has achieved its initial success.

HOW HARD IS ONLINE FUND-RAISING?

Raising money for politics through the Internet posed fewer obstacles to campaigners in 2000 than online advertising. Giving online was less susceptible to the general collapse of Internet activity, if for no other reason than that fewer trend-sensitive intermediaries were required to consummate the transaction. Campaigns could reach donors directly or with the help of political list providers, no ad agencies or media organizations required. That the Internet did not reach all members of society counted as a liability but less so for raising money than for distributing messages and amassing votes. Those who were technologically advanced mainly belonged to the wealthier, more educated, and more politically active segments of society, the same (overlapping) subsets traditionally preferred by fund-raisers.[23] Indeed, the demographic composition of the online population may have presented campaign money seekers with a bonus: political donors have tended to be older citizens, whereas the Net reaches young and middle-aged people at school and work better than direct mail and telemarketing.

There were fewer complexities to online fund-raising than advertising. Even with a middleman firm rounding up digital prospects, there could be little confusion regarding fund-raising goals and results and hence the cost-effectiveness of such brokers. When an ad agency promised "lift" in brand recognition, the benefits were abstruse, even in the unlikely event of log file and survey data to bear out a claim of success. When a fund-raiser promised a boost in dollars donated, the money either came to the client or it did not. Additionally, for those campaigns that paid or took the trouble, the computerization of online donation forms reduced the cost and hastened the process of complying with local, state, and federal regulations. (The cost of procuring and installing such forms was offset by savings in data entry and data-checking labor.) Thus, online money was not only there to see, it was ready to spend sooner. Score two pluses for the process.

This left privacy and spam as a concern, and it was actually a larger one for fund-raising than for advertising. Donors to campaigns, especially at the high end, have been accustomed to a minimum of public attention combined with a maximum of special attention from the recipients of their largesse. The Internet is not helpful in either regard. As discussed in Chapter 2, it makes financial disclosure information easily available, thereby exposing big and big-name contributors to more public scrutiny. Meanwhile, no amount of customized, even personalized, language a campaign could lavish upon a financial contributor through the Internet could match personal contact in making that supporter feel special. The Internet does not look like a good medium to procure big donations. That may turn out to be a civic virtue.

Still, if pseudo-intimacy works in direct mail to net small and medium donations, it should work for e-mail as well. The proponents of online fund-raising had three advantages to cite for political clients:

1. *The cost of online solicitation decreases as the number of solicitations increases.* Once the fixed costs of setting up a communication and transaction system, compiling a donor list, obtaining access to other lists, and composing messages have been paid, the marginal cost of sending out the next appeal for money is practically nil. If a request for money has been couched in general terms, then overkill is the only reason not to ship it to everyone on a campaign's lists, every week of the campaign.

2. *Online fund-raising allows for donor-motivated transactions.* Like ATMs, Internet campaign banks accept deposits at any hour of the day, from anywhere on earth, in seconds flat. The marginal cost of processing online donations is less than nil: that is to say, it is a source of profit, to the extent that the money arrives in compliance-ready, labor-saving forms and the campaign tags its entrance times and routes for the purpose of feedback analysis.

Skeptics such as veteran direct mail specialist Hal Malchow have wondered whether people ever go online in search of a place to donate money to. On at least two occasions in the 2000 election cycle, they did, giving to MoveOn.org and the McCain for President campaigns. These instances are described in Chapter 5.

3. *Online fund-raising allows success to be converted quickly into spending money.* Internet donors can act on impulse and contribute to a campaign before the flash of passion sparked by an appeal or news cue has a chance to subside. This is especially true for direct donations and those mediated by Internet service providers, omnibus portals, and other organizations that already have billing information in their databases.

On balance, then, the case for Internet fund-raising beneath the fat-cat level seems strong. The conventional wisdom among professional political fund-raisers in late 1999, according to one news report, anticipated that "every major congressional campaign will have a fund-raising presence" online in 2000.[24] As with advertising, however, the potential and the predictions went largely unrealized. Journalist Ryan Thornburg, in research conducted for the Democracy Online Project, discovered that only 15 percent of House candidates in 2000 installed an online fund-raising capability on their Web sites. Of that minority, only 20 percent (or 3 percent overall) actively requested contributions; the remaining 80 percent just had a button that said "Contribute." As for donors, Thornburg's limited but suggestive survey research indicated that online donors tended to be the same people who gave elsewhere.[25] No one had tapped the nonsenior strata of the well-off, well-educated online population. E-Contributor, the leading provider of online fund-raising software to the public affairs sector, said it had processed about $10 million in online contributions to five hundred election, advocacy, and nonprofit clients in the two years of its existence when it was sold in September 2001.[26] (An estimated $4 billion was amassed by election campaigners alone in 2000.)

All they have to do is ask, one senses, and online fund-raising will become as common as online research. Campaigns will learn to ask by video and voice as well as text and will have celebrities ask on their behalf (as in the taped messages that pop up in American voice mail boxes near Election Day). Fund-raisers will sell tickets to special events and stage eBay-esque auctions. (The DNC took a step in this direction with an art auction in 2000.) Meanwhile, consumer experiences in e-commerce will break down resistance to entering credit card numbers into online forms.

BCRA AND THE NET

The new Bipartisan Campaign Reform Act (BCRA) exempts the Internet, for the most part, from restrictions on fund-raising and advertising. The early buzz in Washington, D.C., among political professionals alternated between referring to "the Internet loophole" and "the Internet advantage." The loophole will become relevant should the courts uphold the ban on certain kinds of ads paid for by soft money on broadcast media in the days before an election. The Internet could well become by default the channel of choice for last-minute, big-buck attempts to swing an electorate.

But the cyber-exemptions do not necessarily undermine the reform law. Weaning American politicians off large contributions from corporations and unions is a major purpose of the legislation.[27] Since money raised online is likely to come from individuals, and not so much rich individuals as socially active ones, the fund-raisers helped most by the advent of the Internet are those with a network of contacts. They can now round up fifty friends to write $2,000 checks almost as fast as one person can write a $100,000 check. (Fast money is important in politics for the impressions it makes as well as the time-sensitive goods, such as ads, that it purchases.) The Net empowers candidates, in the sense that they thereby need devote less time to fund-raising.[28]

Procedural reforms are notorious for unintended consequences. The 1974 campaign finance reform law spurred an unexpected proliferation of PACs. No one can say what type of fund-raising entity will take off in the wake of the 2002 law—but whether it is controlled by individuals, interest groups, parties, political professionals, or fashionable ideas (that is to say, by popular impulse instead of by an institution), the Internet can be pressed into service. This already is evident from the success stories, and near success stories, of online campaigning in recent years.

5
CASE STUDIES

This chapter tells five stories of online politics. The first two review the use of the Internet by Republican presidential candidates George W. Bush and John McCain in 2000. The third looks at MoveOn.org, a highly innovative and remarkably potent online political action committee that rose to prominence during the Clinton impeachment process and resurged in the months prior to the 2003 war in Iraq. The fourth discusses Web White and Blue, a civic initiative featuring a "Rolling Cyber Debate" among seven candidates for the 2000 presidency. The fifth story uses the "Instant Response Meter" developed by the online public affairs company SpeakOut.com as a springboard for an examination of the Internet as a vehicle for direct democracy.

THE BUSH CAMPAIGN'S ONLINE LEARNING CURVE

Doing well on the Net, let alone on the Web, was not the key to winning the presidency in 2000. But the design and management of the Web sites of presidential candidates still merits review. Because of the incomparable visibility of those vying for the presidency, what happens on "the road to the White House" affects standards in campaigning for other elective offices, as well as for lobbying, governing, and public relations campaigns. The strategy and tactics of the winner are especially influential.

The Bush campaign's early experiences with the Web illustrate the susceptibility of campaigns to the new vagaries of performing in a networked environment, where the tiniest of moves can register around the world in a very short time. The Bush campaign's online miscues may have accounted for some of the lag in politicians' migration to the

Internet. But Bush's team was not deterred by cautionary tales. It kept at online politicking and learned fast and well from its mistakes. By campaign's end—that is, the battle over the Florida vote—it had integrated the Internet into its communication strategy and tactics with beneficial results.

SWATTING AT GADFLIES

When he ran for reelection as governor of Texas, in 1998, George W. Bush basically ignored the Internet. The campaign Web site was pathetic, in marked contrast to the outstanding Net operation mounted by his brother Jeb in his successful race to become governor of Florida. But Jeb had a close race. George W. had a fifty-point lead in the polls and an astronomical lead in fund-raising, just as he would have in the race for the 2000 Republican presidential nomination.

The Bush presidential campaign Web site, www.georgewbush.com, was launched just three and one-half months after the conclusion of the gubernatorial campaign, in March 1999. The campaign purchased more than 125 domain names in an attempt to forestall embarrassments (for example, the Bush team owned "bushsucks.com") and direct traffic to the correct site.[1] But 125 was not enough. In May 1999, an online politics entrepreneur named Ron Gunzberger announced on his Web site, www. politics1.com, that the Bush campaign had purchased Web addresses for a quartet of potential Republican tickets, pairing the prospective nominee with Governors John Engler of Michigan, George Pataki of New York, Tom Ridge of Pennsylvania, and Christine Todd Whitman of New Jersey. An aide to Bush rival Steve Forbes promptly pointed out that three of the four "veeps-in-waiting" were prochoice (all but Engler). The news media noticed the absence of Elizabeth Dole and John McCain from the list. The Bush campaign performed damage control, blaming the purchases on an "enthusiastic young" assistant. The moral was that even seemingly invisible Web activity can be noticed by researchers, and the activities of a presidential front-runner will definitely be scrutinized.

The name-registration story was nothing compared to the www. gwbush.com affair. In April 1999, the Bush campaign sent a cease-and-desist letter to the creators of a parody site with the aforementioned address, which had copied aspects of the official campaign site. The parodists, whose spokesperson and official owner was a young Massachusetts computer programmer and union organizer named Zach Exley, responded by revising their site. It now looked less like the real thing, but the contents were harsher: Exley posted a photo of Bush next to a woman incarcerated for illegal drugs. The Bush team was at this time fending off press questions about the candidate's alleged use of cocaine years before, and the photo juxtaposition incensed them. On May 3, 1999, they filed a complaint with the Federal Election Commission (FEC). It accused gwbush.com of libel and sought to have the site comply with regulations applicable to PACs.

The FEC would reject the complaint in April 2000. Yet even had the campaign won before the regulatory commission, that would have been poor recompense for the problems the filing itself brought down on it. Calling in the government only won the parody site more traffic and public attention than it ever could have achieved on its own. Then, on May 22, 1999, when a reporter asked Governor Bush about the site, he slammed its creators as "garbage" and said "there ought to be limits to freedom." Which, of course, resulted in still more publicity for the parodists. They began to sell T-shirts with the "limits to freedom" line. They collected money to help run negative television ads against Bush. Parody material poured in over the digital transom, and some of it was posted, including a composite photo of Bush with a coke spoon up his nose. As of August 2003, www.gwbush.com was still in operation, as part of another enterprise lampooning Bush administration initiatives.

The Bush campaign's thickheaded and thin-skinned behavior might have worked had Ron Gunzberger and Zach Exley been in the print or broadcast media. A tough public statement by a campaign spokesperson, a few phone calls to government and corporate executives, and the embarrassing information could have been eliminated. But in the decentralized and rambunctious milieu of online politics, efforts to squelch material already released seem destined to backfire. The Bush campaign would have fared better by remaining silent, whereupon the offending material would have vanished on its own accord, washed away by the remorseless tide of online information. Alternatively, the campaign could have responded in kind, putting the governor's renowned sense of humor to good use. Either move would have demonstrated to the online public that George W. Bush could take criticism in stride, that he understood, as all great democratic leaders do, that no public figure is more important than the discourse.

Instead, Bush came across as a bully, and the two free-lancers were in business. (Gunzberger's site also continues to operate.) But the campaign learned the lesson. It soon peppered the FEC with questions seeking clarifications about online campaigning. In October 1999, the Bush campaign Web site was hacked; a communist hammer and sickle appeared on its home page. But that disappeared quickly, and more important, the campaign did not make a big deal out of it. That same month, new personnel began to improve the Net operation. Version two of the Web site appeared on October 18, 1999, with approximately one thousand pages of content, much of it segmented by states, and a pop-up box soliciting donations.[2] Had these features been in place three months earlier, they might have maximized the good publicity Bush garnered for winning what has become known as the "money primary."

THE MONEY PRIMARY

On June 30, 1999, candidates for president filed financial disclosure reports with the FEC. Two weeks later, they sent the FEC the names of donors to their campaigns. Candidates have been providing this information to the agency on a regular basis since the 1970s. But in the summer of 1999 the filings became a campaign event. Candidates sent out last-minute fund-raising appeals, telling their supporters that they needed to make a good public impression. Obligingly enough, the press gave the filing statistics the "horse-race journalism" treatment, describing in headlines who was ahead of whom, and by how much, in dollars and donors collected.

The front-page news, in turn, affected public perceptions of the candidates' relative standing. On the strength of his record-setting $37 million take, Bush appeared to all the world to have an insurmountable lead in the race for the Republican nomination. As for the Democrats, Vice President Al Gore's lead over former Senator Bill Bradley was smaller than expected: $18 million to $11 million. Shortly after the first set of numbers surfaced, Congressman John Kasich dropped out of the Republican contest. Another Republican at the back of the pack, former Tennessee governor Lamar Alexander, said, "Something is wrong when the system doesn't permit an articulate, thoughtful man of John Kasich's stature to even get to the starting line of the presidential race: the Iowa caucuses [slated to begin on February 7, 2000]."

But a new starting line for the presidential race had materialized; the financial report disclosures constituted a "money primary." The Internet was instrumental to its emergence in at least four ways, each emblematic of a cyber-charged acceleration in the dynamics of political publicity and perception. First, the Internet's high-speed, high-volume, low-cost capacities enabled the FEC to collect and distribute financial information in a matter of days. Previously, this had taken weeks, even months. The federal government likes the Internet so much as a data acquisition channel that it now requires presidential and House candidates to file financial information electronically. (The Senate has mischievously exempted itself.) Second, the same constraint-busting qualities of the Internet enabled the press to trumpet the "race results" almost instantaneously with the FEC's release of the information. Since no media outlet had to pay a fee or assign a reporter to obtain the data, each could easily report it as news.

Third, the Internet met a long-standing need of presidential candidates to get a jump on their competitors. Shrewd campaigners have been moving the campaign "starting line" backward in time for decades. Defenders of the New Hampshire primary used to complain about its loss of stature as "first in the nation" to the Iowa caucus, much as Governor Alexander lamented the caucus's loss to the money primary. Fourth, the archiving and organizing capacities of the Internet made it easier for investigative reporters, campaign staffs, scholars, and citizens to search the financial disclosure data for patterns in candidate-contributor connections. In addition to opensecrets.org, described in Chapter 2, half a dozen other sites enable Web users to follow the money (indeed, www.followthemoney.org presents campaign contribution data at the state level). Having analytical stories to write expands the visibility of the event.

As a result of these technological advances and vocational adaptations, a regulatory filing requirement now garners political attention comparable to a (nontelevised) debate. Presidential campaigns now routinely appeal for funds and spin the results in connection with each quarterly financial reporting deadline in the year prior to a presidential election. The March 31, 2003, filings by declared candidates for the 2004 Democratic presidential nomination lacked the dramatic impact of the June 30, 1999, money primary. But that was because no candidate burst away from the others in the tally of dollars collected, no stunning pattern was discerned in examining who gave money to whom, and the entire topic of presidential politics was overshadowed by the war in Iraq. The June 30, 2003, money primary was another matter. As described in the preface, it marked the emergence of the Howard Dean campaign's ascendancy.

George W. Bush amassed so much money in the first half of 1999 that he could forgo the presidential matching funds and the regulations associated with them. This made him vulnerable to populist attacks as the big-money candidate. But the Bush campaign anticipated that criticism and used the Internet to counter it. GeorgeWBush.com posted the names and dollar amounts of every individual who contributed to the campaign, even if the amount was beneath the FEC reporting threshold. After the money primary, the campaign pointed with pride to the 74,000 individuals named on its Web site, 41 percent of whom (30,663, to be exact) donated $200 or less. In sum, Bush's victory in the Internet-fostered money primary intimidated opponents. His disclosure initiative immunized him against charges of swamping campaign finance reform with fat-cat contributions. For 2004, the Bush reelection campaign Web site posts contributors in a searchable database.

THE HOME STRETCH AND THEN SOME

As the long campaign continued into 2000, the Bush team developed state-by-state online news release operations to fill the templates established in the second iteration of their campaign Web site. Days before the Republican convention, on July 18, 2000, Bush released a television ad touting yet another "reopening" of his Web site. New features included "GWBTV," the capacity to distribute videos, and a semiautomated content management system enabling more campaign staffers to add new material. Yet the technical improvements may not have been as important as the campaign's recognition that ubiquitous promotion enhanced online campaigning. The primary audiences for the site were supporters, the press, and leaders of the high-tech industry. On the same day the ad was released, Bush met with 350 members of his high-tech "advisory council," an assemblage of big-name endorsers and big-time donors. Both the ad and the meeting were touted in a news release.

If Bush wanted to be known as Net-savvy with selected audiences, he saw no need to trumpet that image to the electorate. The Republican presidential nominee never mentioned his Web site address during his acceptance speech in Philadelphia—nor, for that matter, during any of his fall debates with Gore. Campaign spokesman Tucker Eskew suggested that Bush regarded such a reference as tacky, akin to reciting an 800 number and saying operators were standing by.[3] For reasons that remain obscure (and obtuse), Al Gore never mentioned his Web site during his acceptance speech or debate statements, either. As noted in the first chapter, these convention and debate silences had a severe impact on online political journalism ventures.

In the fall, the Bush-Cheney campaign, as it had become over the summer, purchased online advertisements featuring an interactive tax calculator, a device used by Republican James Gilmore in his successful 1998 bid to become governor of Virginia. "How much will the BUSH TAX CUT save YOU?" read the banner ad. A click on the banner brought the calculator onto the viewer's screen; the viewer entered income, marital status, number of children, and the percentage of income from a second earner, and back would come a dollar figure. The calculator also sported a link to the campaign Web site.

The Bush-Cheney campaign continued to dispatch personalized messages to e-mail supporters by issue interest, geographic location, and activist history (that is, donors received customized appeals gratefully acknowledging their past contributions). On September 14, the campaign began an e-mail list expansion drive, called the "e-train," in which supporters were exhorted to contact friends via e-mail on behalf of the campaign. The first such missive predicted the closest election since 1960, when the margin between Kennedy and Nixon wound up being less than one person per precinct. The e-train added 100,000 new addresses in its first month.[4]

The October 2 presidential debate marked the first time presidential candidates attempted to integrate online content with a live televised event. The Gore campaign chose the occasion to trot out its Instant Messaging (IM) operation, whereby debate viewers could communicate with large numbers of other people in real time. But while the service collapsed under the weight of its own complexity, the Bush campaign's special Web site, www.debatefacts.com, performed brilliantly. Both sides assailed the factuality of the other's claims; however, the Bush criticisms were keyed to actual remarks Gore made, while the Gore messages were prepared issue statements keyed to the topic being discussed. The Bush site automatically refreshed itself with new content, while visitors linked to the Gore campaign via the Web or IM had to click for themselves. The Gore campaign made it easy to forward those statements to friends. But with titles such as "Squandered Years," it was hard to know what they were referencing. The next morning, under the title "Take the Gore Invention Tour: Pick Your Time or Topic," the Debatefacts site offered thirty-two crisp entries contrasting Gore statements with documentary evidence. Each entry was indexed by the time Gore said it and the subject matter. Bush's policy positions were accessible on the right-hand side of the page.[5]

The Bush campaign's Internet operation remained active during the dispute over the Florida vote, providing news updates and attracting

$2.4 million in funds from more than eighteen thousand donors. As staffer Wesley Wilson pointed out, the dollar value to the campaign was even larger since it expended nothing to attract people to the site or send out e-mail appeals.[6] (The Gore site did not send out an e-mail until November 26, out of concern for FEC regulations.)

It seems safe to conclude that the Bush campaign brain trust could not help but be impressed with the powers of the Internet. At the start, George W. Bush needed a Web site good enough not to embarrass him before political and high-tech elites and, thinking more positively, lively enough to impress the fraction of his supporters who visited its pages. By campaign's end, the Web site and accompanying e-mail outreach were a tangible asset. This incremental appreciation of value is probably more characteristic of campaigners' experiences with the new medium than the quantum leap of success enjoyed by John McCain. But that leap was launched from a platform built through incremental progress, as a review of the McCain campaign and two precursors makes clear.

THE CYBER-FLIGHT OF MCCAIN 2000

In early February 2000, the John McCain for President campaign benefited from a surge of online popular support unprecedented in scope and significance in the brief history of Internet politics. The campaign did not just "bounce" upward after McCain won the New Hampshire primary, as winners there have done for decades. For a few weeks it flew.[7] As word of McCain's victory in the February 1 primary spread, money starting gushing into the campaign Web site at a rate of $30,000 per hour—this according to the campaign, which cleverly fed bulletins on the phenomenon to news media, which in turn reported it, which generated more donations. After four days, the total topped $2 million, a rate of almost $21,000 an hour. More than a week elapsed before the frequency of donations slowed to less than one every four minutes (and that first four-minute-plus interval occurred between 2:00 and 3:00 A.M.).[8]

In all, the McCain campaign said it raised $6.4 million through the Internet, 27 percent of its entire funding.[9] Since much of it came in contributions of less than $250—the average online contribution was $112—the campaign reaped an additional $4 million in matching funds from the federal government. It also enjoyed a huge influx of volunteers. The McCain e-mail list rocketed from 60,000 before the primary to 142,000 afterward, constituting 80–90 percent of its volunteer base. As a result, wherever McCain wanted to go, a corps of volunteers was there ready to advance and populate the events. Thanks to e-mail, the volunteers could be identified and introduced to one another within days.

The McCain campaign was close to broke the day of the New Hampshire primary. The online infusion of money, volunteers, and publicity kept it alive for another few weeks, which included primary victories in Michigan and Arizona. The Internet enabled the campaign to convert "momentum," a rhetorical asset commonly associated with election winners, into more concrete political resources quickly, before it could dissipate. This would not have happened to the extent it did had the McCain campaign not explored the possibilities of the Net during the previous year and prepared to capitalize on just such a big moment.

HOW IT BEGAN

The McCain online operation began in February 1999. It was conceived as the virtual headquarters for a long-shot candidacy. Max Fose, a political aide to the Arizona senator for eight years, had daily responsibilities, along with fellow Arizonan Wes Gullett. Dan Schnur, a Californian who served as communications director for the campaign, also was a vital part of the Internet team.

Gullett had traveled to Minnesota to meet with Phil Madsen of the Jesse Ventura online campaign. The 1998 race run by Ventura under the Reform Party banner is a tricky one from which to draw solid generalizations about online campaigning. It took place in an uncommon electoral environment: Minnesota law limits campaign spending and permits same-day voter registration. The candidate, already a figure of some fame, did not need to devote many resources to getting his name and persona recognized. The gubernatorial contest was a three-way race, and the major-party nominees beat each other up to the Reform candidate's benefit, especially in televised debates. Ventura also gained support from a terrific series of television advertisements.

Still, Ventura would not have won without the Internet. His online campaign illustrated the political importance of the non-Web aspects of the Net, especially e-mail. Anyone who sized up the candidates in the 1998 Minnesota gubernatorial race from the quality of their Web sites would have dismissed Ventura; his Web site looked crummy, while the Web sites of Democrat Hubert Humphrey III and Republican Norman

Coleman were sleek. But Web site appearances deceived. Out of necessity and antiestablishment instinct, the Ventura campaign concentrated its energies on the "Jesse Net," its e-mail network of more than three thousand supporters and, more widely, on the networks of professional wrestling and Reform Party enthusiasts. These intersecting networks enabled the campaign to communicate with itself, to reassure supporters and inform the public at a critical moment that a quotation attributed to the candidate (regarding legalized prostitution) was not true, to coordinate and beef up attendance at an end-of-the-campaign rally, and to increase registration and turnout on Election Day.[10]

Although they did not realize it, another precedent for the type of virtual guerrilla campaign McCain would run online existed. It was the campaign of a gay man whom the local press would label "Jesse Ventura in heels."[11] In the summer and fall of 1999, Tom Ammiano, a member of the San Francisco Board of Supervisors, pondered the idea of an underdog campaign for mayor against the incumbent, Willie Brown. Two challengers to Brown, former Mayor Frank Jordan and multimillionaire Clint Reilly, seemingly left little space for a fourth credible candidate. But there was yet room to the well-known and well-funded trio's left. While Ammiano temporized, supporters created a Web site for him, www.runtomrun.com, and collected more than two thousand signatures on a petition to that effect. Three weeks before the election, Ammiano entered the race. The network of supporters zoomed into action, instructing people how to write the candidate's name on the ballot, exhorting them to download signs and place them in windows. The Ammiano campaign spent only $25,000 but vaulted its candidate past his rivals into the runoff against Brown (who would win the runoff decisively).

McCain encouraged his Internet team to experiment. He told them he wanted to try new things and have fun.[12] McCain trusted Fose and Gullett because they were long-standing aides. Computer geek volunteers or political consultants with a vested interest in online politics (such as those the McCain campaign would contract with, Virtual Sprockets and Hockaday-Donatelli) would not have had the latitude to try and err that the Arizona loyalists did. Fose and Gullett devoted six weeks to planning, one month to programming, and once the Web site opened, four to six hours a day to maintenance.

McCain quickly came to believe in the power of the Internet. His feelings were reinforced when Fose showed him how much their Web site traffic spiked when the candidate gave out the URL on CNN's *Larry King Live* on October 13, 1999. Thereafter, the senator did not just mention the Web site whenever he spoke, he invited people to go there, embracing his essential role as driver of traffic, the best first step in the publicity chain.

Every day, Fose walked around campaign headquarters collecting information for the site. The McCain site had the most features of any of the top eight primary-season presidential candidates, according to Web watchers at the Annenberg School of Communication of the University of Pennsylvania. Actually, it was a cluster of sites that would grow to eight in number. This occurred for no particular reason; the McCain campaign was careful to promote the URL of only one site, the main one, in its standard publicity. The issues pages attracted the most traffic. But the key was the underscored calls to action appearing on many pages of the site and in e-mails. They were often quite specific: we need money for a radio ad buy (after sending out the ad as an audiofile preview to those on the list); watch McCain on MTV; join in a chat on iVillage (a commercial site); view the list of more than $13 billion in wasteful and low-priority congressional pork barrel spending items; visit the Web site today and please e-mail the headquarters with your opinions about the changes in the navigation tools.

In December 1999, the campaign realized it needed help procuring signatures to get on the ballot for the Republican primary in Virginia. At a cost of $1,500, it purchased a microtargeted ad buy, sent for one week to commercial Web pages likely to be viewed by Virginia registered voters. The online ads persuaded 198 viewers to visit the campaign Web site (a 2 percent click-through rate). Ninety-seven of them became signature gatherers, a 49 percent conversion rate. McCain's name appeared on the ballot. In January 2000, Fose issued a request on the Web site and via email for volunteers to make ten phone calls to strangers who happened to be registered independents and Republicans in New Hampshire. Eleven hundred people enlisted within six hours. After a week of this, eight thousand calls had been completed and tabulated. Fose had invented the interactive phone bank, which more than ninety-two hundred volunteers would staff for the duration of the campaign. Cost of volunteer transportation, room rental, phone equipment, line leasing, supervisor, and donuts: zero. Worth to the campaign: priceless.

New Hampshire, like Minnesota, allows same-day registration for voting. More than thirty-eight thousand Granite State residents took advantage of that option on February 1, 2000. There is no telling how many of them voted for McCain, but chances are quite a few did. There also is no telling how many McCain voters were moved to show up and register by an online message or a personally delivered message logistically facilitated by the Net, but again, chances are that quite a few were. The campaign expected to win and prepared for a postvictory spike in online traffic by spending $30,000 on additional equipment to field it. The decision was controversial within the campaign; McCain personally approved the expenditure. Victory came, and with it, the cyber blast-off.

On February 10, the McCain campaign staged an online fund-raising event, selling five hundred "admissions" at $100 each. Four aides sifted through hundreds of submitted questions and handed a few to the candidate's wife, Cindy, who read them aloud so the candidate could respond in kind. "Attendees" with high-speed connections could watch live, while those connected via dial-up modem could hear the senator and look at graphics and text. The event was taped by CNN for at least three of its shows; other media came, too.

On February 22, while celebrating his victories in the Arizona and Michigan primaries, John McCain waved a *Star Wars* light-saber toy. The campaign would have been smart to adopt that as its symbol—provided, of course, that George Lucas and his lawyers approved. By associating himself with Luke Skywalker, McCain framed his battle with George Bush in a way likely to evoke warm memories and the urge to spring into action. If anyone watching on television experienced that Star Wars rush and wondered how to act on it, the placards McCain supporters were waving told them: www.mccain2000.com.

Then the McCain campaign sputtered. The candidate said in a speech that he did not need two giants in Virginia politics, Pat Robertson and James Gilmore, to win there. When he failed to make good on the boast, he seemed less a Skywalker than a braggart. Online appeals to California voters, complete with instructions on how to proceed in that state's open primary, did not get the job done. The battle for South Carolina turned nasty. As February ended, Fose could see the number of volunteers and donations plummeting. The last favor the Net did for the campaign was inform it that the flight was over.

Nothing that happened to Ventura or Ammiano compares with the rush the McCain campaign received. Could such a scale-busting momentum boost occur in a nonpresidential campaign? Certainly any candidate can prepare for a traffic spike and use it to collect a lot of money and attention in short order, as well as to embellish an underdog, populist image. However, only the presidential primaries contain a sequence of elections in a compressed time frame. Candidates for other offices will have a harder time sustaining Net-fueled momentum in terms of generating votes.

The McCain for President online operation did not cease when the campaign ended. The Web site became a platform for campaign finance reform and other McCain issue initiatives under the name "Straight Talk America." By 2001, when the McCain-Feingold campaign finance bill passed the Senate, the Arizonans' Internet operation had metamorphosed into a grassroots lobbying and political action committee. Fose and Gullett, who had absorbed and transcended the lessons of JesseNet, also had learned from MoveOn.org.

MoveOn: The "Kumbaya" PAC

From both a strategic and a democratic perspective, the most impressive online mobilization force to surface in the United States to date is based at www.MoveOn.org. In the space of two years, 1998 to 2000, MoveOn matured from a record-setting publicity magnet into a unique breed of pressure group: a citizen action portal that blends the community spirit of grassroots movements with the sophisticated tactics of a PAC. In 2002 and 2003, MoveOn became the first (and, as of this writing, the only) political organization to repeat the feat of leading a significant grassroots campaign through the Internet. MoveOn stands out as the prototype for such organizations in the digital age. It advances civic engagement and public choice as well as the causes and candidates it advocates.

Grassroots Politics and the Internet: Not as Simple as It Seems

Grassroots organizers recognized early on that the Internet was a godsend. In 1996, Ed Schwartz, a Philadelphia-based activist, was able to distill his successes with e-mail into a how-to book entitled *NetActivism*.[13] Environmentalists and human rights activists embraced online communication in those years. They faced the difficulty of conveying complex cases to people on a global scale congruent with the problems they were concerned about, yet they lacked the financial resources commanded by their corporate and governmental opponents.[14] The Net met their needs.

In awarding the 1997 Nobel Peace Prize to Jody Williams and the International Coalition to Ban Landmines (ICBL), the prize committee observed:

> The mobilisation and focussing of broad popular involvement which we have witnessed bears promise that goes beyond the present issue. It appears to have established a pattern for how to realise political aims at the global level.[15]

The ICBL campaign became an inspirational touchstone for online organizers and commentators. How else but online could a Vermont activist have progressed from a passionate idea to an international treaty and Nobel Prize in just five years? However, the "pattern" recognized by the prize committee had more to do with the formation of a gigantic coalition of nongovernmental organizations than with the Internet. E-mail saved the antilandmine campaign money and helped it move faster. But it did not bring together the thirteen hundred organizations in more than eighty countries. That was assembled largely by means of the fax machine and face-to-face meetings facilitated by the jet plane. The ICBL campaign did not turn to e-mail until 1995.[16]

The true lesson of this famous case is that the Net helps grassroots campaigns just so much. On the one hand, the new medium facilitates the organizing and deployment of supporters. It alerts people, equips them to contact decisionmakers, and keeps track of all such activity with clockwork precision and speed. On the other hand, the Net does little to help grassroots campaigners recruit support. Its contact directories are incomplete, and online advertising is problematic. These drawbacks will lessen in years to come. But it will remain hard to motivate people through the Internet, from joining a campaign to giving it money to being willing to express themselves in public forums.

Indeed, the Net may put advocates at a relative disadvantage when it comes to inspiring political action. Compare online rallying with the traditional rally environment of an auditorium or plaza. The traditional settings benefit from the Aristotelian unification of action with time and space. Speakers can be seen and heard by those they are attempting to rally—as can, very often, symbolic objects of intended group opposition or support. Anyone who thinks about leaving early must risk the glares of the assembled, while those who fall in line will bask under the heat lamp of solidarity. Online motivators, in contrast, must rely on whatever currently can be placed within reach of the universe of computer screens. The words, images, numbers, and sounds will come through with sufficient fidelity to be understood by whichever members of the target audience choose or happen to come across them. But what about the emotional subtext? Communicating emotion through the Internet absent the palpable signs of a group assembly is the advocate's enduring challenge.

CENSURE AND MOVE ON

In December 1998, at a Harvard University conference on online politics, a Berkeley, California, entrepreneur named Joan Blades held forth for a few minutes on her vision for the Internet. She spoke about returning power to ordinary citizens, moving politics beyond confrontation, and the glories of community. It struck some in attendance as fuzzy-wuzzy. When she finished speaking, another panelist, Republican operative (and now online newsletter author) Rich Galen, cracked, "Kumbaya.org." The back of the room collapsed in laughter.

No one was laughing six months later. MoveOn, run by Blades and her partner Wes Boyd, raised $250,000 in a five-day burst before the June 30, 1999, FEC filing deadline. That set a record for online fundraising. Within a year, both the Bill Bradley and John McCain presidential campaigns would exceed that total. But Blades and Boyd were not famous candidates running for high office. Nor were they executives of an interest group, party, union, trade association, or corporation, with organizational funds and members to draw on for political purposes. They spent no money on marketing, advertising, or polling. People found MoveOn by word of mouth. They contributed money because they agreed with the campaign's message. And they joined the organization because they embraced its mission and approach.

In September 1998, Blades and Boyd created an online petition to express frustration with the impeachment process. The message embodied in their original Web site title, "Censure and Move On," resonated with individuals who, while not forgiving of President Clinton's moral transgressions, nevertheless disliked the Republican response to those sins. More than 100,000 signed the petition in the first week. By the 1998 midterm election, 300,000 had signed. The day before the House voted on impeachment the count stood at 450,000, and MoveOn had begun collecting pledges for money and volunteer time to defeat in 2000 those who voted for impeachment. Five million dollars in pledges rolled in the day after the House vote (a Sunday). In early February 1999,

MoveOn announced that it had collected $13.4 million and 750,000 volunteer hours in pledges.

Petitions and pledges constitute mostly symbolic force. Blades and Boyd wanted to go beyond that. They selected candidates to support in thirty congressional races in 2000. In many of those contests, a challenger favored by MoveOn stood a good chance of unseating a pro-impeachment incumbent. The Berkeley couple reengineered the MoveOn Web site so that visitors could easily read about each race and then donate money to any or all of the endorsed candidates; an individual entered FEC contributor and credit card information, made selections from the virtual slate, and received an instant acknowledgment and thank-you letter directly from the designated campaigns, in whose accounts all of the money was deposited. (MoveOn still to this day does not solicit or accept contributions by check.)

By Election Day 2000, MoveOn had bundled and distributed almost $2.4 million contributed by more than forty thousand Americans, about $60 per person. One of the challengers, Jean Elliott Brown in Florida, began her involvement as a MoveOn volunteer, delivering petitions and generating local press coverage during the impeachment process. She lost. But thirteen of the thirty won. MoveOn was the top contributor to Adam Schiff, who unseated House impeachment manager James Rogan in a California House race in which millions of dollars were spent. (Statistics on bundled volunteer hours were not available.)

MoveOn had generated political power out of the disgust individuals feel when elected officials act wrongly under the spotlight of a big news story. This is nothing new. Dispersed emotional similitude has been a common social phenomenon since the advent of mass communication and especially broadcast communication, which lends simultaneity to the experience of a situation the grassroots campaigner aspires to tap. Millions of individuals in a time zone laughed in sync at *I Love Lucy* and cried at John F. Kennedy's funeral.

Waves of feeling with political ramifications are not new, either. Now and then a mass media-triggered sentiment has manifested itself in polling results, that, when publicized, have affected the balance of forces in a political struggle. For example, in 1974 millions of Americans flocked to read uncut compilations of Watergate tape transcripts, ignoring President Nixon's convenient and well-promoted "summary" of what he had said to his aides in the Oval Office. Transcript readers, encountering a vulgar, ruthless, and self-preoccupied character referred to as "P" instead of the familiar televised image of the president, came away from the text with a less favorable opinion of the man by a three-to-one margin, according to a May 5 Gallup poll.[17] This undirected but unmistakable flow of popular scorn hastened Nixon's fall from power.

A generation later, during the next impeachment struggle, the House Republican leadership made public the report of Independent Counsel Kenneth W. Starr on President Clinton's salacious behavior, about which he testified before a grand jury. Again, the desire to read about possibly illicit and decidedly secretive Oval Office activities stirred tremendous popular interest in a political document. This being 1998 and not 1974, the Starr Report was released online. The wave crested faster. AOL recorded more than eight hundred thousand downloads in the first twenty-four hours.[18]

There was, however, no concurrent swing in public opinion. The Clinton depicted in the Starr Report was not as shocking a contrast with his public image as was the case with Nixon. A different type of Oval Office activity was involved, in a different economic and political climate. On the tactical level, the House Republicans did not place a sign-up box for petitions, contributions, and e-mail addresses on their Web site at the same time the Starr Report was posted on the Library of Congress site.

MoveOn neither created nor publicized the news story on which it capitalized. Instead, it rode an emotional swell by expressing an opinion not well represented in the partisan cross fire over Clinton's conduct and by creating a simple outlet for others who shared that opinion to join them in bringing it to bear on the relevant political struggle. This use of the Net to take a stand on a big issue in a space left unoccupied by established figures and institutions was MoveOn's first great innovation. In a sense, Blades and Boyd rode the same kind of audience energy burst that humorists vie to tap when they react to the news. But whereas comics and satirists fill a void in the public discourse by daring to say what no political authority can afford to say for fear of antagonizing a portion of the electorate, MoveOn played it straight. And it took names, e-mail addresses, and zip codes.

If big news can provide the emotional push to get a great many people into a Net campaign in a short time, what can raise emotions between headlines? Political fund-raisers know one answer to that question: the next election. It is never too early to ask people for money to prepare for the next battle against the other party. In an era where the starting line of candidacy declaration and engaged competition moves ever backward and the press keeps score on funds raised, the case for early fund-raising appeals grows easier to make. Early money purchases first impressions for a campaign; incumbents use it to project invincibility and challengers rely on it for name recognition. Political players with early money to spread know that their largesse constitutes a great favor that candidates may find difficult not to repay, the universal concern with perceptions of being bought not withstanding.

MoveOn's second great innovation was to use the Net to broaden the early donor pool. MoveOn is a registered PAC, licensed to influence elections through the disbursement of campaign contributions. But it has inverted the customary PAC funnel of power by permitting those with the dollars to decide where their money will go. In so doing, MoveOn distinguished its appeal from most of the other PACs seeking to tie the next election to the most recent big struggle. It gave its members strategic information and choices. It made them feel like players because they were, in fact, playing the game like big contributors and professional political operatives do.

The entity MoveOn most resembles is EMILY's List, a PAC dedicated to the election of prochoice women to Congress. EMILY's List pioneered the tactic of bundling donor choices into sizable contributions to a slate of candidates. It experienced a rush of publicity and recruits after the Supreme Court confirmation hearings of Clarence Thomas, in which Anita Hill, who had accused Thomas of sexual harassment, defended her reputation before an all-male (and all-white) Senate Judiciary Committee. EMILY's List has thrived but has not benefited from a second surge keyed to a news event. MoveOn did, in an entirely different issue domain from its first success.

IRAQ: MOVEON'S NEXT WAVE

MoveOn sought to broaden its issue portfolio before the 2000 elections and continued to do so thereafter, with limited success. In May 2000, Blades and Boyd collected 60,000 signatures to a "Gun Safety First" petition launched after school shootings in Colorado. For the 2001–2002 cycle, MoveOn's members selected campaign finance reform and protection of the environment as priority issues. In August 2002, the organization had the e-mail and regular addresses of 350,000 people in its main database. This represented a 22 percent decline from its peak. It reported $1 million in expenditures, with a mere $127,000 distributed to forty-four House and Senate candidates.

Like many Americans, Blades and Boyd were distracted from the midterm elections. That fall MoveOn focused on opposing U.S. military action in Iraq. It took the lead in the online campaign for a coalition of approximately three dozen organizations, united under the rubric "Win Without War." The coalition eschewed the guerrilla protest techniques developed by the antiglobalization and corporate boycott movements, concentrating instead on the construction of a network with which to pressure officials through conventional channels.[19] A MoveOn "action campaign" page in October quoted four conservatives against the war (Brent Scowcroft, Henry Kissinger, Senator Chuck Hagel, and House Majority Leader Dick Armey) and linked to a page with a sample letter to Congress, a form to transmit "to your email circle," and requests for volunteer help and financial support. The most sophisticated option offered a petition template to be presented by MoveOn to the president and Congress "at appropriate times in the policy making process." MoveOn controlled the timing and dominated the language of the citizen petitions, while participants controlled the privacy of their e-mail addresses.

By this point, MoveOn had opened an office in the nation's capital. It expanded its staff to six, including Zach Exley, the man who had gotten under the Bush campaign's skin with gwbush.com. It commissioned a television spot—a re-creation of the notorious "Daisy" ad run by the 1964 campaign of Lyndon Johnson for president in which a young girl plucking flower petals dissolved into a nuclear mushroom cloud, conveying the message that a vote for Goldwater ran the risk of nuclear war—and a buyer to book the ad on commercial television. The week before the 2003 Super Bowl, MoveOn learned from its media buyer that the station carrying the game in the Washington, D.C., market had a cancellation. On Thursday, MoveOn alerted its members, asking for $40,000 to air the spot during the game.

The success of this initiative inspired similar calls to action in the arena of commercial advertising. A "local ads" page on the MoveOn Web site featured the facsimile of a newspaper advertisement entitled "Experts Say: Iraq—AlQaeda/There's Simply No Link." Quotes from experts spelled out the argument symbolized on the page by a broken chain. Next to the advertisement on the Web page, MoveOn listed the names of 111 newspapers in small- and medium-sized U.S. cities, along with the cost of placing the ad down to the penny (ranging from hundreds to thousands of dollars). Meanwhile, members received customized e-mails with the names of the five newspapers closest to them, along with a link to the Web site page. These listings included a space where the amount raised to date would appear, as a further incentive for citizen action. The "telethon" ploy proved unnecessary. All 111 ads were over-subscribed within twenty-four hours. MoveOn turned to billboards and raised thousands of dollars in a similarly short span to put the "No Link" ad before American drivers. However, the Viacom Corporation refused to post them. In all, more than $1.3 million was collected to pay for citizen-distributed antiwar ads between December and February.

On February 26, MoveOn staged a "Virtual March on Washington." This was not so much a lobbying effort or demonstration as a bid for publicity, there being no war resolution before the Congress at that time. Participants signed up to phone, fax, or e-mail their senators and the White House and were given assigned time slots to meet the stated goal of having each Senate office receive a message every minute of the work-day. Bypassing the House meant that this would require 48,000 contacts instead of 256,800, an easier goal to meet. As it turned out, more than 440,000 calls were scheduled, and estimates of the number of calls and other contacts actually made topped 1 million. MoveOn attempted to compensate the Senate staffers and interns saddled with logging the onslaught of messages by sending them popcorn via Federal Express, but packages do not get delivered to Capitol Hill as they did before the 2001 anthrax episode. The "march" made the news media. Jay Leno referred to it, and AOL linked to it from its welcome page.

The Virtual March and related activities caused the membership of MoveOn to zoom past a million. In early March 2003, it sponsored an emergency petition to the member states of the UN Security Council (1 million signatures in five days). The Win Without War coalition staged a candlelight vigil (3,000 localities in 100 countries), and MoveOn posted digital photographs and comments. As the war began, MoveOn offered words of praise and consolation to its members, concluding: "No one has ever said that waging peace is easy. It may take days, or months, or years. But moving forward together, we will make history. Thank you for all you do." Then, after the war, on April 24, it dispatched an e-mail to its virtual community that included the following:

> We'll throw out Bush and the Republicans using every means available: by registering a wave of new voters, by organizing to make sure they get to the polls on election day, by raising enough money to compete with the President's mountain of special inter-

est money, and by volunteering for political campaigns. We'll make it easy for you to play a part.

President Bush believes he doesn't have to listen to the American public—which, even during war, has overwhelmingly been skeptical or strongly resistant to the idea of an American empire. He has decided that his faith in the military takes precedence over his faith in democracy. The election in 2004 is our chance to take our democracy back.

With that, MoveOn began another news-wave-to-citizen-action transition. This time, it likely will gain force from the development of a bridge technique, which marks the third grassroots innovation. MoveOn has figured out how to give its members continuous opportunities to take small, simple steps and see the results in a matter of days, if not hours. Help pay for this ad to go in that newspaper. Go to this vigil and bring a candle. This pointillist style of political action improves on the concrete requests issued by Ventura and McCain in that the gratifying result often appears in other venues besides the one directly affected. Individuals daub a dot on a canvas—more literally, they click on a button—and the dots create a picture displayed before appropriate decisionmakers and the general public. The "painting" experience and finished work attest to what political scientists term "efficacy." So do MoveOn's accompanying e-mail narratives, which caption the pictures. The citizen-artists are encouraged to believe their efforts have an impact, which increases the likelihood that they will try again.

When the Iraq war began, MoveOn's list stood at 2 million members, 1.3 million in the United States. If two statistics from the 2000 cycle hold true in 2004—the ten-to-one ratio of members at the news story's apex to donors for the ensuing election cycle and the average donation of $60—the MoveOn PAC will have almost $8 million to bundle off to candidates in 2004. That amount of money would have put it third among overall donors in the 2002 election cycle and first among PACs by better than a two-to-one margin. (The top PAC donor, the National Association of Realtors, handed out $3.65 million.)[20] Furthermore, with the right technical and legal engineering, 2004 campaigns could count this money as direct individual contributions, and not as PAC donations.

MoveOn's developments of news-surfing, donor-directed funding, and pointillist rhetoric have enabled it to motivate grassroots political action. It is as though Blades and Boyd said "Kumbaya that" to conservative activists. Oddly, no mirror organization has emerged to join

MoveOn in ideological combat across the gamut of issues. Perhaps that is because grassroots action works better in opposition—and the conservatives are in power.

Web White and Blue and the Challenges of the Online Debate

The Net and Debates: Added Considerations for Campaigns and Sponsors

Candidate debates stand out from all other events that occur during election seasons. Campaigns interrupt their competitive outreach activities, and the candidates enter a setting their organizations do not control. They face off against each other for what is likely to be the only time before the election, and they cannot turn for help to their staffs, their colleagues, or even their notes in many instances. They submit to rules that their representatives have had a hand in designing but that also reflect the interests and bargaining skills of their competitors and the debate sponsors (often a consortium of news media organizations and civic groups). And they are expected to speak seriously and substantively about the issues facing the electorate, as their questioners see those issues.

Why do campaigns consent to put their candidates in these situations? A candidate may be up for the challenge, committed to the ideal of a policy dialogue conducted in public view, or perhaps goaded into participating by the press and opposition. (Those fellows who show up in chicken costumes at the campaign rallies of debate holdouts are agents of the public good.) But the fundamental incentive for candidates to debate is the prospect of reaching a large and attentive audience. People gather for debates and talk about them afterward. The theatrical setting promises the simple excitements of personality contests and game shows, as well as the intricate drama of a clash of wits, wills, ideologies, and ideas.

Debates usually entice less interested and less committed members of the electorate into the campaign arena. The unusually large audience, combined with the volatility of the proceedings, give debates the potential to shake up voter preferences in sufficient numbers to affect election outcomes. Yet, even when debates do not trigger decisive swings in voter preferences, they can tilt the results by lifting and sinking morale among campaigners and by convincing opinion leaders in the media, parties, interest groups, and elsewhere to shift the terms in which they discuss the race. Moreover, debates can affect the images of candidates, issues, and the political system well beyond the elections for which they were held. Ask Dan Quayle.

The possibility of a big change in poll status and the perceptions of authoritativeness, the confrontational setting, the time limits, and the intellectual demands all put debaters under tremendous strain. The sight of individuals dealing with crisis situations reinforces the propensity of people to remember decisive moments and general impressions from debates for years and years. The high stakes also may be one reason why American campaign debates typically have no judges. None of the parties to a debate seems to want one designated group of observers to wield such concentrated influence. Instead, all sorts of commentators and survey populations weigh in with assessments.

A debate, in sum, presents a campaign with a triple challenge: to shape the event's format and expectations, to have the candidate perform in a manner consistent with both strategic considerations and his or her own sense of self, and to dominate the interpretive free-for-all.

The challenge is somewhat different for the sponsors of a debate. They must balance the needs for sizzle and substance. A debate without substance violates its central purpose, which is to provide the electoral process with an intellectual component and to enhance the capacity for rational deliberation, dialogue, and choice, on a community if not an individual level. No one expects candidates to don rep ties and take either the affirmative or the negative side of a resolution. Yet, strip away the regulated back-and-forth and side-by-side position taking on policy matters, and what remains would not be worthy of the word "debate" in Oxford, Maryland; Oxford, Mississippi; or Oxford, England. Debate sponsors want to live up to the relaxed definition.

A debate without sizzle, however, will not get a big enough audience to justify a sponsor's expenses and efforts. Normal commercial calculations do not apply; in this instance, the media want big ratings because that likelihood is what gets the top candidates to participate and the mainstream press to attend. (Clever incumbents with more to lose than gain by debating sometimes push for a boring format. That way, they protect their leads, yet have a credible response to the critics in chicken costumes.) The normal recourse in American life of those staging such forums is to inject sizzle by casting celebrities and by encouraging speakers to shout, hurl insults, adopt extreme positions, and otherwise be edgy. Yet that recourse would not be worthy of the word "debate," either. To sponsors, therefore, a debate must blend the best that seminars, on one hand, and talk shows, on the other, have to offer.

The Internet expands the ways in which a debate can be constructed. The Net can accommodate a larger number of candidates, including minor-party and unaffiliated ones, within the same time span. It makes longer debates feasible, with more time to deliver and consider questions, answers, statements, and rebuttals. It allows more nonparticipants (campaign researchers, journalists, experts) to join media-featured "spin room" commentators in issuing remarks on candidate answers immediately. It even permits a selection of instant comments to be looped back to moderators and panelists before the debate ends, so that the comments can be incorporated into follow-up questions. It makes it possible for multiple groups of people to act as judges, in large numbers, and rate candidate performances in short order, for the debate as a whole and for different parts. Finally, the Internet enhances the capacity of individuals to learn from debates by linking clips and transcripts to contextual material.

Of course, more debate features do not necessarily yield a better debate. The Internet makes it harder to focus on, and to verify the authenticity of, individual debate performances. No one outside a campaign wants anyone other than the candidate to participate during the debate—yet no one wants to watch a candidate peck out a statement on a laptop, either. The wider range of questioners and judges adds to the moderator's burden. Citizen comments can be as tedious, hyperbolic, digressive, loopy, and wrong as those of debaters, without high stakes and a sense of performing under pressure to redeem the audience's experience of enduring them.

Still, it would be a shame if the Internet were not quickly integrated into the tradition of campaign debates. Fortunately, in this aspect of electoral politics, as in others, the trials and errors of Net adaptation have begun.

THE ROLLING CYBER DEBATE

In the fall of 2000, seven presidential campaigns were invited to participate in a "Rolling Cyber Debate" under the auspices of the Markle Foundation's online politics initiative Web White and Blue (WWB).[21] Each of the seven candidates had legally qualified to appear on enough state ballots to win the 270 electoral votes requisite for becoming president. The format called on their campaigns to answer a question of the day from the citizenry; as a reward, the Rolling Cyber Debate afforded them space for a message of the day and for rebuttals of the other campaigns' answers and messages. All contributions were unedited and unrestricted with respect to media mode (that is, campaigns could submit text, sound, video, links, and so forth in any combination). The debate lasted from October 1, 2000, until Election Day, a total of thirty-seven days (with Sundays off). It was accompanied on the WWB site by "Best of the Best," which from June 2000 onward summarized and linked to news media stories about the presidential campaign. A third part of the site publicized information compiled by nonprofit institutions about the presidential campaign, and a fourth consisted of directories to state-by-state information about registration and voting.

WWB began as a destination portal and public affairs directory in 1998, www.webwhiteblue.org. In 1999, the president of Markle, Zoe Baird, announced that the foundation would focus exclusively on Internet projects for the next three to five years. Markle recognized that a directory to campaign sites would be superfluous for 2000, with the emergence of for-profit Web sites to fulfill that function. The foundation set out to create a forum pegged to the presidential contest that politicians would want to participate in, that the news media would want to report about, and that would both involve and benefit citizens in a timely manner. Leading members of the WWB team included Douglas Bailey, campaign adviser to President Ford in 1976 and founder of the insider political news service "The Hotline"; Steven Clift of Minnesota E-Democracy, which staged the first online candidate debate; Barbara Fedida, formerly of ABC News; Michael McCurry, former White House press secretary for President Clinton; and Shabbir Safdar and Jonah Seiger of Mindshare Internet Campaigns.

WWB's political content initiative resembled several other nonprofit initiatives, most notably DNet (short for "The Democracy Network"). DNet began in the summer of 1996, devised by the Los Angeles–based Center for Governmental Studies. It has bounced between the private and nonprofit sectors and will be run by the political directory firm Capitol Advantage in the 2004 cycle. DNet consists, in the main, of a searchable set of matrix boxes known as the "issue grid." The DNet issue grid presents candidates for an office down the vertical axis and issues selected by the sponsors—or, refreshingly, by the candidates themselves—along the horizontal axis. Each cell contains either a link to candidate issue statements, signified by a checkmark, or the debate equivalent of the empty chair, a "no comment." The more checkmarks a candidate offers, the higher his or her row appears on the issue grid.

Badgering candidates to participate is labor-intensive, and DNet has partnered with the League of Women Voters to do that. Over time, DNet has expanded the number of elections it covers and has developed the capacity to display audiovisual answers. In 1999, before its transfer from the Center for Governmental Studies to the firm Grassroots.com, DNet won a favorable ruling from the Federal Election Commission creating a legal space in which online debates could be managed without running afoul of corporate contribution restrictions. For the year 2002, DNet recorded twenty million page views from more than a million visitors, who stayed on average more than seventeen minutes to peruse the entries for more than 25,000 candidates and 680 ballot measures nationwide.

Although DNet encourages campaigns to expand their questions and answers over the course of an election season, it has faced the same campaign antipathy to questionnaires that besets Project Vote Smart, described in Chapter 2. Consequently, DNet has resembled a static voting guide more than a dynamic debate. That is a valuable resource for a representative democracy to have; all the same, I have not been able to find an instance where a campaign used its answers for DNet's grid to significant political effect (as, for example, Newt Gingrich used C-SPAN in his rise to Speaker of the House of Representatives.)

The WWB team wanted to have both civic and political impacts. It hoped for a lively debate that would feed minds and make history. WWB sought to meet the interrelated, although asymmetrical, challenges of boosting candidate and news media interest in its online debate through two innovative wrinkles. First, the Rolling Cyber Debate attempted to import some of the sizzle of live events by imposing daily deadlines on the campaigns. Second, instead of posting the contents of the Rolling Cyber Debate and related WWB features exclusively on its own site, the Markle Foundation put together a network of seventeen heavily trafficked Internet sites, including news organizations (CNN, *New York Times*), content aggregators (MSN, Yahoo), and specialty portals (iVillage, NetNoir). These sites, with a reach to 85–90 percent of the online American public, agreed to carry WWB content as a syndicate. This audience maximization served as the candidate lure, while the promise of top candidate/campaign participation served as an incentive for the syndicate members. With both the campaigns and the media on board, the public, in theory, would follow.

There were two high points in the Rolling Cyber Debate. On opening day, October 1, 2000, candidates responded to a question from "Joe of Tulsa": "What is the most important issue in this campaign?" The answers were as basic as the question—too basic, perhaps, to qualify as news. But they were substantive, linked to details, open to challenge from other campaigns, and in those respects invaluable to the citizenry, which could access them for five weeks prior to the vote. Indeed, the array constituted a good setup for journalists seeking newsworthy comments from the campaigns. On October 17, 2000, the question of the day solicited views on the issue raised by the Napster case. The answers constituted fresh news and reverberated through the online politics community.

In the main, however, the cyber debate never really got rolling. The closeness of the Bush-Gore contest may have dampened the campaigns' willingness to take chances with provocative answers, any one of which might have sparked a multicandidate exchange. The candidates did not use the WWB forum to elaborate on statements from their televised debates. Neither did the news media, although the *USAToday* Web site linked from its news story "Candidates Set to Spar Tonight" to WWB, providing a model of how online and televised debate content could connect via press coverage.

Substantive disappointments aside, the signal value of the Rolling Cyber Debate and WWB was that the participation incentives worked. Bush and Gore stayed the thirty-seven-day course, along with John Hagelin, Patrick Buchanan, and Howard Phillips. Harry Browne dropped out, dissatisfied with his third-tier placement on the debate home page. Ralph Nader never participated (because, some WWB team members surmised, that would compromise his image as the excluded candidate). Most of the seventeen syndicate partners stayed the course, too. In postelection interviews, representatives from these online firms expressed approval for the cooperative arrangement. Since WWB 2000 was a veritable "plug and play," it did not drain their resources, and no other campaign material had to be sacrificed to make room for it. As for the public, traffic was low: 738,000 page views for the debate; 3.9 million for "Best of the Best"; 7.5 million overall. By comparison, CNN reported 2.2 million page views during the ninety minutes of the first televised presidential debate. However, multimethod social science research conducted by Arthur Lupia of the University of Michigan for Markle found that citizens exposed to WWB returned in high proportions on their own, learned from what was presented there, and felt more confident about politics as a result.

WWB demonstrated that syndicated distribution of content can bulk up media or sponsor power enough to induce normally cautious favorites to participate in a debate forum. At the least, syndication gives sponsor representatives a shot at coaxing candidates into such an arena. WWB also taught that campaign participation will go slack—they will "mail it in" instead of e-mailing what is hoped for—without the pressures of a verifiably big audience and live interaction. The Rolling Cyber Debate did not test candidate skills in memorable ways. At this writing, there are no plans to revive WWB for 2004. If that happens, the team should include someone from the Commission on Presidential Debates (CPD). It makes little sense to conduct separate debates on television and in cyberspace.

In 2000, the polling firm Harris Interactive designed a predebate survey for CPD that allowed visitors to the CPD Web site (www.debates. org) and a collection of nonprofit sites to fill out a questionnaire and thereby suggest questions for the first presidential debate. A postdebate survey reprised the topic questionnaire and added an evaluative element regarding the candidates' performances. This foray into engaging members of the online citizenry in the before and after stages of debates should be pursued. For example, it would be technically simple to allow the public to rank proposed questions to be put to the candidates, and it will make for a nice flourish to have a citizen pose the top-ranked question during the debate. Since 2002, Major League Baseball has allowed online fans to fill the thirtieth and final spot on the All-Star Game rosters in this fashion from among five nominees. A February 2002 poll conducted for the Pew Debate Advisory Standards Project found that 51 percent of voters would be at least somewhat likely to go online to vote on proposed debate questions.[22]

Increasing citizen participation in pre- and postdebate politicking would, of course, enlarge the audience for the debate itself and thereby reinforce the participation incentives for campaigns and sponsors. It would be compatible with the much-derided (perhaps unjustifiably so) public or civic journalism movement, which encourages news media organizations to treat their readers as sources.[23] Such additions to the debate format also would be one of many ways in which online technology could conceivably advance the cause of direct democracy without prejudicing the political values that direct democracy can impair through poor design and execution. As the next case demonstrates, online expressions of direct democracy can be confusing.

THE INTERNET AND DIRECT DEMOCRACY

COUNTING

Computers are, in essence, counting machines. Counting has long been at the heart of democracy, too, requisite to the determination of majority preferences. In the summer and fall of 2000, the apex to date of public experimentation in online media politics, a smattering of ventures in political counting surfaced on the Web. Each of these electronic counts purveyed a mechanism by which members of the public could instantly register their opinions on a current issue and the results could be seen instantly, or soon thereafter. The counts, which keyed off the presidential nominating conventions and debates, were in effect variations (preludes, echoes, counterpoints, riffs) on the delegate roll calls and the general election. But, in some respects, these rapid computations had less to do with the making of the next president and national agenda, or with the sorts of professional research described in Chapter 2, than with the entertainment business. They would be at home on commercial television as well as the Web.

Dial-response mechanisms track audience reactions to messages. Audience members watch the message and twist their wrists so the dial in their hands reflects the thoughts and feelings in their heads along a like/dislike continuum; the pulse of their responses is then aggregated with those of others. This feedback technique has been part of commercial and political opinion research for decades. As a child in Los Angeles in the 1960s and 1970s, I can recall being invited to a building in Hollywood called "Preview House," where we were shown a "control" cartoon with Mr. Magoo before being asked to react to television pilots and advertisements.

During the 2000 national political conventions, the political start-up company www.speakout.com trotted out an "Instant Response Meter," in which the mouse and keyboard replaced the dial. Site visitors were invited to rate convention speeches on a scale of 1–100. Results were posted on the site the morning after the speeches. The graphic display of the aggregate ratings was handsome; one could see at a glance how the color-coded spikes and arcs in the responses of the populations matched up with specific passages from the speech texts. (It would be no great technical challenge today to match responses to audio and video clips as well.) The analysis that accompanied the display was tentative and shallow, for example, "Messages aimed at female voters appear to have hit their target." But then, analysis did not seem to be the major purpose behind the Instant Response Meter. To make money and put its business on a solid footing, SpeakOut.com needed as many participants in and viewers of its counting device as possible. The firm sweetened its invitation to home page visitors to rate convention speeches by dangling a $5,000 prize for one lucky participant. This pitch sacrificed some control over the audience's composition; the respondents consisted, to an indeterminable degree, of people interested winning money. The absence of any prohibitions on voting more than once also ceded control over the sampling.

If self-selecting samples were an accurate gauge of the populations they mean to represent, then Alan Keyes, whose core supporters swamped online polls with multiple responses, would have been giving the GOP nomination acceptance speech. SpeakOut.com tried to finesse the self-selection warp by weighting the data; that is, it arithmetically jiggered the counts so that the participants would resemble the voting population. Weighting is a common practice in survey research. But it works well only when the demographic characteristics being adjusted correspond to the questions being asked. This population was asked to react to every topic that came up in an address but was weighted only by gender, age, party preference, and likely vote. No wonder SpeakOut.com published no margin of error statistic. It was incalculable.

The Instant Response Meter was more devoted to promotion than research. There is nothing wrong with that, especially in connection with a national political convention. (Now that primaries decide nominees, it could be argued that *every* aspect of the contemporary national political convention, official and nonofficial, is promotional.) But SpeakOut.com, conceived as a political information portal, was at that time shifting its business model toward that of an online message-testing service for campaign and market researchers.[24] It would soon change its name to Ntercept, an allusion to "mall intercepts," a common recruitment method for dial-response sessions. The company thus acted at cross-purposes. The value of the Instant Response Meter was whipsawed by the change in organizational mission. Both SpeakOut.com and Ntercept perished.

AOL's 2000 convention package featured surveys rating the speeches and another kind of counting exercise, in which AOL members chose questions to be posed to guests on its nightly "pregame show" Web-cast. Nonmembers of the ISP giant could view the show at the public AOL site, but only members could participate in the surveys and question selection process. This activity was not passed off as research. Rather, it was interactive infotainment: sign up for AOL and join in the fun of collectively interviewing a talk show guest. The majority rocks!

In the fall, on MSNBC, Republican political consultant Frank Luntz conducted a "postgame" show that mixed elements from focus group, dial-response, and television talk show sessions. As moderator/host, Luntz was wont to tease out observations that ratified his conservative preferences. For example, after the third presidential debate, Luntz asked thirty-six "undecided voters" to raise their hands if they thought George Bush "did better than you expected he would." Most did. Luntz's earlier pronouncement, "We have a clear winner in this debate," thereby seemed verified. Luntz's partisan affiliation went unmentioned by MSNBC anchor Brian Williams. All this disturbed the American Association for Public Opinion Research (AAPOR), which issued a news release condemning the spectacle.[25]

More counts were being tabulated by Dick Morris, arguably the preeminent political strategist in America during the mid-1990s. Morris flouted the convention for professional consultants by maintaining simultaneous ties to top politicians in both parties (notably Bill Clinton and Trent Lott) and by publishing strategy memos in the paperback edition of his autobiographical account of those years.[26] For the 2000 cycle, he brought out a book and for-profit Web site with the same name: vote.com. In *Vote.com* the book, the author puffed up the significance of online interactivity with populist rhetoric. On vote.com the site, first-time registrants were eligible for 1,250 award miles on major airlines.

The storefront feature of vote.com invited Web users to send a collective message to the authorities. "We always e-mail your vote to key decisionmakers," read a home-page slogan. The topic of the featured vote of the day could be a current issue, but it also might be popular entertainment. During the Democratic convention, visitors were asked to rate Gore's convention speech, and the results were sent to the DNC and the vice president. Three days before that, the topic was "Are the Clintons Taking Too Much of the Spotlight from Gore?" There was no space on the online voting form for individual comments; the message to authorities consisted solely of the vote results. As with many interactive counts, participants could click through to see the latest totals.[27] A vote.com discussion area could be accessed by giving the Web site one's e-mail address.

Morris needed as many people and as diverse a population of message-senders as practicable in order to market the data he collected about them to advertisers on his site and to public affairs clients. The data included standard demographic categories as well as type and size of employer/business and what might be called issue groups (so that a vote.com client could purchase access to, say, people who voted in a vote.com poll for or against the death penalty). Vote.com continues to operate today.

What are campaign professionals—and the rest of us—to make of these four countings by SpeakOut, AmericaOnLine, Frank Luntz, and Dick Morris? One way to answer the question is, of course, by counting opinions. Since 1998, survey research has documented the popularity of online polls; in 2002, 32 percent of those using the Internet for political information and action registered an opinion through an online poll. This was the most common mode of online political engagement by a considerable margin, well ahead of sending political e-mail (17 percent), taking part in discussions and chat groups (7 percent), and contributing money to a campaign (5 percent).[28] Campaigners in 2002, however, had yet to embrace the Internet as a channel for testing the popularity of their messages. A survey found that testing messages was regarded by campaign managers as the least effective of nine online applications they were asked to assess.[29] Taken together, these findings suggest that campaigns will be able to build support among the online citizenry by giving them more opportunities to voice their opinions of current ads, agendas, and activities. But this does not begin to exhaust the implications of online countings for democratic politics. As the four examples show, there is a myriad of forms and contexts in which such soundings may manifest themselves.

VOTES, POLLS, AND POPULARITY CONTESTS

One context stretches back to the origins of democracy in ancient Athens. Can the voice of the people be trusted in public affairs? Political philosophy has pondered that question since Plato and Aristotle. The historical expansion of popular participation in U.S. governance supplies a second context, albeit an oblique one. The right to vote has been extended by race, gender, and age; the scope of voting has been widened to the Senate and, in some states, to referenda, initiatives, and recall. This movement has of late turned to the convenience of voting: easing registration procedures, encouraging voting by mail, and so on, based in part on the idea that extending conveniences will sustain the trend. Visions of government by electronic referenda have been a part of the

American democratic discourse since the debut of the computer.[30] Should a serious push for electronic voting, petitions, and the like swell up in society, it will be the next wave in a series of largely successful agitations to enlarge citizens' involvement in the steering of the state.

Opponents and skeptics of direct democracy, as the movement is known, worry about the costs in policy stability, rationality, coherence, and flexibility. There is only so much detail a populace can be expected to assimilate before casting a vote, even online, where a great deal of information can be made proximate to (and, conceivably, viewing it can be a prerequisite for) the virtual pulling of the lever. Yet, conversely, can anyone else's voice—experts, the moneyed, safe incumbents—be trusted to rule over the people? Advocates of direct democracy regard instant, policy-specific, and binding popular votes as a political cleanser that can wipe out corrupt deals between elected representatives and special interests.

In order to take a side in this perennial debate, as it applies to the Internet, one must have a sense of the facts and circumstances of online countings. Yet one quality the four prior examples have in common is that their counts occurred so fast as to obscure the assumptions on which they were based and the purposes to which they were put. A counting with online elements is no faster than one on television, and in that sense it presents nothing new. But, as with online debates, new complexities are introduced into the basic format.

Consider a fifth example. Google News consists of a continuous computerized culling from more than forty-five hundred news sources "without regard to political viewpoint or ideology." The "frequently asked question" page explains:

Q. How does Google decide what stories are published on the Google News homepage?

A. The headlines on the Google News homepage are selected entirely by a computer algorithm, based on many factors including how often and on what sites a story appears elsewhere on the web. This is very much in the tradition of Google's web search, which relies heavily on the collective judgment of web publishers to determine which sites offer the most valuable and relevant information. Google News relies in a similar fashion on the editorial judgment of online news organizations to determine which stories are most deserving of inclusion and prominence on the Google News page.[31]

Google would no sooner disclose the algorithm by which journalistic choices have been compiled and weighted into Google News than Coca-Cola would put the chemical formula right on the can. One can respect the company's proprietary concern yet still wonder what this means for public affairs if Google News catches on as well as its companion search engine has. Is there really such a thing as unbiased news? And if there is, of what value is it in orienting citizens and politicians? Google News is crystal clear compared with the sorts of counts that campaigns solicit. By 2004, the Luntz show might well feature a crawl on the bottom of the screen attesting to thousands of online and telephone "voters" agreeing that the Republican debater performed "better than expected."

In order to gauge the potential effects of countings, one must be able to discern their fundamental nature and aims. Consider Table 5.1, which distinguishes votes from polls and popularity contests.

With a sense of these basic types in mind, one can look at the mechanics of a count and the rhetoric used to interpret it to make inferences about its impact. The SpeakOut Instant Response Meter, seen in this framework, could be the precursor of a tool that both political and media

Table 5.1 Types of Counts

	Votes	Polls	Popularity Contests
Eligibility	Qualified and willing participants	Designated populations	Whoever obtains access
Quality controls	Law, government, civic surveillance	Scientific method, peer review of results	Sponsor administration
Purview of results	Binding decisions on voters as well as entrants	Systematic evidence for arguments, theories, and strategies	Awards for voters and entrants or diversionary information
Attendant goods	Peaceful transfers and transformations of power, community solidarity	Knowledge	Fun, sponsor publicity, and profits

professionals will deploy at those moments when politicians are making big public impressions (at conventions, debates, hearings, news conferences, and so on). But, as has been the case with overnight polls, it is unlikely that one company will try to please both political and media professionals with the same online meter. The politicians will work behind the scenes; their targeted subpopulations and interpretations will remain confidential. The media will continue to let everyone in who wants to play with the mouse and will settle for superficial interpretations.

This was AOL's approach, with access to celebrities serving as an incentive to expand membership. Any knowledge generated would be incidental and in the fun-facts vein of quiz shows. Any impact on civic and political engagement would derive from changes in the participants' and onlookers' comfort level with the moderator and guests. The MSNBC show was similar except for the involvement of Luntz, who appropriated popular culture forms for ideological purposes. On television, the sight of "undecided voters" raising their hands in praise of Bush carried a symbolic subtext; on the Web, that sight might well be accompanied by links to a campaign Web site.

Dick Morris transcended the direct democracy debate, much as he straddled the partisan aisle in his consulting business. His site promised participants a shot at political influence as well as a chance to see how their opinions stacked up against others on a question of the day. (One has to wonder, if Morris really wanted to enlighten the Clintons about how his vote.com voters felt about their appearance at the 2000 Democratic convention, whether he would have bothered to use e-mail to reach them.) In his book, Morris predicted that the Internet "will inevitably return our country to a de facto system of direct democracy by popular referendums. The town-meeting style of government will become a national reality . . . the real town meetings will occur on the Internet, with real people, and the politicians will have to listen."[32] On the other hand, Morris concluded, the more society embraced online voting, the more voters would recognize their mistakes and defer to experts.

THE PREPONDERANCE EFFECT

Motives and purposes aside, the Internet has contributed to public confusion over political countings in another way: by multiplying how many of them accompany big news events and how many loom over politics on a daily basis. As many critics have noted, infotainment never stops; it has become the ambient condition in which civic and political activity occurs. And while infotainment is easy to detect, especially when the media go "wall-to-wall" on a single story, it is not so easy to resist. It is worth contemplating whether, through sheer profusion, networked computers will bring audience participation in popularity contests (and such knowledge-seeking opinion polls as happen to receive news media coverage) to a point where the totality becomes indistinguishable from electoral behavior.

Even when majority preferences in such instant surveys do not acquire the force of law, they might serve as a powerful stand-in for public opinion. Writing before online polling, political scientist Susan Herbst worried that polling had eclipsed direct popular action, because poll results "give the illusion that the public has already spoken in a definitive manner."[33] The Internet enables entrepreneurs to "go high definition" with that illusion, conveying the actual speech of discussants along with tabulations of voters. As will be seen in the concluding chapter, cybernetics will allow them to go further and represent both discussions and tabulations over time in a recursive framework that, unfolded over time, can suggest campaign momentum, civic learning, strategic advice, a compelling narrative, or any combination thereof. What cybernetics would automate, in part, infotainment peddlers would contrive as narrative. Imagine one of the four examples above conducted in several iterations as part of blanket coverage, propagating the sense that public opinion is coalescing around (or polarizing) the political struggle of the day. Such narrative simulations are not far off in the future. Early in 2003, the Fox network FX flirted with "The American President," a proposed reality television series in which viewers would use the telephone and Internet to pare eighteen candidates for president down to one.[34]

Political scientist L. Douglas Rivers, the chief executive officer of a leading online polling firm, Knowledge Networks, worries that politicians will become slaves of electronic polls.[35] Some politicians, no doubt, will buckle before digital incarnations of public opinion. But is such behavior new? It is too easy to extrapolate from the latest, undeniably impressive advances in the technology of soliciting audience reactions and to conclude that the history of the Republic is about to become a cacophony generated by the clicking of millions of mouses, with or without a conductor furnishing sheet music and cues. We would seem to be as far from that as we are from the capitulation of free will to artificial intelligence, a parallel vision that reappears every time a computer wins a chess match. Indeed, we may be farther. For there are some awfully big hurdles, de facto and de jure, in the way of government by (Net-powered) audience research, for better or worse.

First, there is rarely a preponderance of sentiment pointing in a single direction. In a paradoxical and perverse way, the presence of flawed and otherwise compromised audience research deprives authentic findings of influence. Happily, though, the reverse is also true. In any situation, a Luntz or an AAPOR could prevail, or they could cancel each other out. Even the undeniably binding power of election results can be sapped by audience research on the same topic; succession to office is almost guaranteed, but a mandate is not. So one reason direct cyber-democracy is unlikely is because Internet-borne public opinion will always modulate, and sometimes muffle, the legally binding voice of the people.

Second, with respect to predictive soundings of public opinion ("horse race" polls, straw votes, and the like), one cannot be as sure in politics as in marketing that the probabilities will work out and people will act or react in the way they said they would. Since voters generally have one day on which to act—in policy battles, that day is rarely well known in advance—outcomes depend as much on mobilization as on anything that can be discovered through opinion research. That the Internet can place a mobilization outlet on the same Web page as a research finding (and a hortatory spin of that finding) by no means condenses learning and doing into an automatic occurrence. In politics, the walk must still be walked after the research reports the talk. Public opinion can be no more than an environmental influence in policymaking.

Third, audience research has a hard time plumbing opinions, intentions, and likely behavior with respect to trade-offs and compromises. Researchers' questions overclarify options and cannot anticipate bargains. Yet most political decisions of a free people in a pluralistic society, particularly under a federalized system of government, are based on such murky derivatives of starting positions. Audience research on politics inevitably yields nonattitudes, conjured up for the questioner so as not to look rude or ignorant. When polls do report attitudes more precisely, they leave decisionmakers with a continuum of opinions and thus negotiating work to do.

What the combination of these three phenomena—the surfeit of data, the gap between expression and action, and the likelihood of unpolled compromises emerging from the policy process—implies is that online tallies, alone and in combination with those taken by more traditional methods, will never be an adequate substitute for political intelligence. Polls, focus groups, response graphs, and interviews can help immensely in message development, but they cannot write the message, let alone translate it into policy. And they do not come with sufficient caveats regarding margins of error. That makes direct democracy impossible. Both its backers and detractors will always be disappointed with public opinion research if they presume it to be tantamount to political action.

6

THE VIEW FROM THE CONSOLE

A LOOK BACK AT EARLY PREDICTIONS

New technologies evoke speculations, which project beliefs into the future. Americans have often folded democratic ideals into their technological speculations. As Langdon Winner notes:

> The building of canals, railroads, factories, and electrical power plants as well as the introduction of the telegraph, telephone, automobile, radio, and television have all been accompanied by enthusiastic proclamations that the innovation would give ordinary folks greater access to resources, more power over key decisions and broader opportunities for political involvement.[1]

In cyberspace, according to democratic optimists, politics will benefit from the hugely enhanced capacity of citizens to find others on a scale and with a speed and depth well beyond that previously possible. James Warren, who successfully lobbied the state of California to adopt government disclosure rules, generalized from his experiences and envisioned "one-shot activism" as a major development in American politics. In the mid-1990s, he predicted individuals and organizations coalescing on an ad hoc basis around issue positions. These digital coalitions would be strong enough to put the positions on the public agenda and would then disband.[2] There might not be a lot of people in them, but precision timing would multiply the force of their voices. Thanks to the Internet, interests did not have to be entrenched to have an impact on elections and policies.

The thunderclaps of political sentiment that empowered Jesse Ventura, John McCain, MoveOn, the globalization protests, and other campaigns either on or below the national radar screen in the late 1990s lent credence to Warren's vision. Using the Net, coalitions can be organized and apply pressure in a flash. These examples tend to be left-of-center and libertarian, inviting the question of whether the coming of one-shot activism has an ideological bias. Do online activists share a point of view, an economic interest, or anything else capable of forming a political movement by virtue of the fact that they are online?

Some in the 1990s speculated that the Internet did bring a movement into being. They regarded the research-oriented, noncommercial origins of the Net as an inherent and irreducible quality that stamped, or could stamp, the political character of those who would master it. "The nature of the nets is such that content matters more than form and substance more than flash," wrote technology-columnist Wayne Rash, Jr., in 1997.[3] Perhaps the apotheosis of civic optimism in Net forecasting appeared in an audience-flattering piece in *Wired* magazine that same year.[4] Jon Katz proclaimed the existence of a "digital citizenry," ballyhooed by the magazine as the new swing group in American politics. "Move over 'soccer moms' and 'angry white males,'" the article began. The archetypal digital citizen "blends the humanism of liberalism with the economic vitality of conservatism." Membership was conferred in terms of "connectedness," that is, digital citizens exchanged e-mail at least three times a week and used at least three of the following: laptop, cell phone, beeper, home computer.

In fall 1997, the date of the Frank Luntz survey to which Katz's article was tethered, membership among the connected constituted 8.5 percent of the U.S. population. That number has certainly increased. But because the results did not control for education, income, or any other variable, the correlation between technology use and political attitudes, behavior, and power was incidental at best, and specious at worst. There was no evidence to support the idea that "connected" people had a shared identity that could make them potent either as policy advocates or as swing voters. A more sophisticated 2003 study of "influentials" established an empirical tie between civic activism and intensive use of the Internet but found only a slight conservative tilt to their views.[5] Perhaps conservatives have not embraced the Internet for political activism as much as the left because they have dominated government and public thinking during these years. As the Bush case shows, they have certainly embraced the Internet for campaign research, communication, and fund-raising.

Not all technological speculation is rose-colored, even in America. Political scientists were quick in the 1990s to counter the optimism of technology activists and those who covered them sympathetically. "The Internet," wrote Richard Davis, "is destined to become dominated by the same actors in American politics who currently utilize other mediums."[6] Outsiders relying on the Internet may gain speed, precision, a penchant for data, and even a pile of newly made money, but they will still lose to established interests and incumbents. Davis saw the Net as the next big mass medium after radio and television. The political establishment would bring order, which most users crave, to the Net, and in so doing win their allegiance during policy fights.

The democratic pessimists conceded that the Internet offered more room and routes than older media for alternative representations of public affairs to circulate. The establishment would lose some control over what gets framed as news and commentary. However, Michael Margolis and David Resnick pointed out that business interests would still pay the closest attention to policymaking and the policy implications of elections.[7] While the Internet set up new channels for political participation, it would not change, in the main, who participates, how often, and how well. As Bruce Bimber put it, "neither the psychology nor sociology of political participation are altered by increasing the capacity of citizens to communicate."[8]

Pippa Norris, a more optimistic political scientist, associated the coming of the Internet with a series of developments she placed under the rubric of "the post-modern campaign." As with other theories of postmodernity, pluralization, fragmentation, and uncertainty are the indicative adjectives, befitting a medium that is multidimensional in its uses and decentralized in the production and consumption of content, trends in mass media conglomeration notwithstanding. In this milieu, professional consultants would "become more coequal actors with politicians" on the strength of their capacity to coordinate grassroots activity.[9] Meanwhile, the apathetic would not become alienated, because the Internet would provide them with politically harmless outlets that the mass media did not. Those of a mind and will to organize could do so. Others, instead of having to watch the evening news in a sullen mood, could head to eBay. Norris is no utopian. But her ironic vision has room for democracy to thrive as a niche activity.

Why Politics Lags

Now that a few more years of online politics have elapsed, these speculations can be reconsidered to see whose beliefs have been confirmed, disconfirmed, or scarcely inflected by the evidence. What is striking is how much falls into the third category. It is still too early to mark any systematic or historical Net-related change in how Americans campaign and how they react and respond to campaigns. Likewise, it is premature to consider whether any issues have gained or lost public force from the Internet, with the important exception of privacy protection.[10] It may remain that way for a while. Politics lags virtually every other professional (and so-called professional) domain in integrating the Internet into its operations.

"Internet Time" has slowed for everyone in the wake of the high-tech bust (except, perhaps, in the laboratories and workshops). Yet, boom or bust, the transition from vision and experimentation to habit and institutionalization seems destined to move more slowly in online politics than in commerce, society, education, or even government. The process of social adaptation requires, in its first phases, a space in which much can be tried, errors can be quickly noticed, and pioneers can move ahead with little penalty for having failed or not succeeded as much as expected.[11] One successful online campaigner told me that "we learned by playing in the space," while the opposite number recalled how the "pressure not to err was intense."

The U.S. winner-take-all election system offers scarce rewards and severe penalties for trial and error behavior in campaigns. At the party level, a landslide victory in one jurisdiction does not compensate for ten losses elsewhere, as it might in the marketplace. At the individual candidate level, learning by doing does not yield sufficient rewards to warrant experimentation, inasmuch as there is no bankruptcy court, rebirth ritual, makeup exam, or civil service protection to cushion a politician's fall from elective office. The current partisan alignment, with official power closely divided, a third of the electorate declaring itself independent, and a small number of contested seats across the country in each election, only magnifies the risks associated with innovation.

Ventura and McCain were political daredevils, celebrities whose renown did not depend on party strength but rather battened on party defiance. They had nothing to lose by experimenting with the Internet. Said Web master Phil Madsen about the Ventura campaign: "For every three people we attracted we drove out two, but that was OK, most of those who stayed were entrepreneurs who knew how to make something out of nothing."

Consider the case of Maria Cantwell, a political wunderkind who spun out of the fast track when she lost her House seat in 1994, only to rocket to wealth as an executive with the Internet company RealNetworks. Cantwell began her 2000 race for a Washington Senate seat intent on breaking ground in online campaigning, and indeed, her Web site's moderated discussion groups did that very thing. Then came the "fish incident." Cantwell's Web master, John Beezer, copied a promotional photo of her incumbent opponent, Slade Gorton, off his Web site. Gorton, whose family founded a frozen fish company, was standing "looking goofy" next to someone in a salmon costume. Beezer thought he was having some fun and making a point about industry ties. The Gorton campaign accused the Cantwell team of intellectual property theft, claiming the photo belonged to them. While no charges were filed, the accusations of theft resulted in the challenger's campaign pulling back from the edge of pioneering. "There's no problem with trial," Beezer reflected. "You just can't afford the error."[12]

The fixed calendar of elections and the rise of the permanent campaign put experimenters in a peculiar temporal bind. On the one hand, client contracts and confidences must be won far in advance; the online campaigner needs time to set up the operation, debug it, and train the rest of the campaign team in its uses before things really start to move. On the other hand, once the bell goes off, campaigns are open for public business only a few weeks every two years or more (before the primary and general elections). The Internet makes it easy to accumulate a great deal of data in these compressed periods of time on how voters, donors, journalists, party officials, interest group executives, and opponents react to online campaign strategies and tactics. But no one yet knows how to analyze such information with authority.

Suppose, for example, that click-stream logs, which detail how long visitors stay on a particular Web page, disclose that a great many visitors have lingered on the campaign "store" page, once removed from the home page of the general site. Does that mean the campaign can make a lot more money offering more items for sale? Or does it mean that, once transported from the main site to the store, visitors do not know how to get back or move elsewhere? This may seem like an innocuous example. However, in the heat of Harry Truman's kitchen where political decisions get made, any hesitation or complication can cost Net campaigners severely, given their low status going into a meeting vis-à-vis the television and poll advisers, with their track records.

And so the state of affairs in the diffusion of online campaigning in 2002 was this: the campaigners were struggling along, and a core of citizen activists was available and in some cases waiting for them. But for politics to move online as fully as other facets of contemporary society, the campaigners and citizens must not only adopt the technology; they must find comfortable ways of connecting with (and disconnecting from) each other.

THE CONSOLE

Even as Beezer and other dot-pols struggled, the first versions of a digital political machine were migrating from the laboratory to the marketplace. The machine could be glimpsed in microcosm by examining its console menu: the array of utilities offered to someone seated before a computer terminal equipped with the right campaign management software. An omnibus console (a composite of actual features on available software) might display the following options:

- Send e-mail to list(s); update, add, or remove list members.

- Post message onto Web site; search message archive.

- Track contributions; file government reports.

- Construct profiles of voters, supporters, volunteers; enable outsiders to view part of their profile and enter comments and corrections.

- Search Web for media coverage; code coverage for analysis.

- Cost out advertising placements and results.

- Detect traffic spikes and security breaches.

- Create custom reports for clients, assessing recent and overall performances in terms of strategic goals.

By and large, the e-campaigners who could work that console, the professional vanguard, lacked seats at the strategy table in 2000 and

2002. Three things have to happen before they can take their place along-
side the pollster, (old) media adviser, chief of staff, and the other top-tier
campaign decisionmakers; online campaigning must become (in no particular order) more visible, adaptable, and readily subject to pricing.

First, the press has to publish success stories featuring dot-pols as
protagonists. Phil Noble of PoliticsOnline looks forward to an election
night when a victorious candidate calls the Web master up to the dais to
share in the credit. (He has been publicly predicting this since 1998.)
Such recognition will spur personality profiles about the James Carville or
Lee Atwater of the Net (especially if, as suggested in Chapter 4, online
advertising was part of the story). Dot-pols from the opposing party will
work the new star's name into their client pitches and will contend that
they can bring similar results to their side.

Visibility will lead to more contracts. But to secure client trust, and
to keep the seat at the proverbial table, dot-pols will also need a set of
routines—a combination of programmable algorithms and battle-tested
instincts—they can quickly adapt to campaign predicaments. Political
situations change constantly, and they can change greatly in a hurry.
Routines will enable dot-pols to read "real-time" developments and make
equally swift recommendations that have the ring of expertise to the rest
of the strategy team. Furthermore, most candidates and advocacy groups
recognize that they are not Jesse Ventura, John McCain, or Joan Blades
and Wes Boyd. Average campaigners in unexceptional circumstances need
reassurances that the Internet can work for them. Routines fill this need
as well.

Adaptability will not help dot-pols, however, if embarking on an
approved course of action drains their resources. Managing a campaign's
online content, its lists, its advertising, and the security of the operation
all demand frequent attention. For example, in contrast to a message
sent through conventional channels, for which the job is essentially completed with its delivery and distribution, an online message that makes a
splash, positive or negative, will generate ripples of communication back
to and around the campaign that will have to be accounted for, adjusted
for, and perhaps answered on an individual basis. Even an online message
that sinks without a trace requires a pathological analysis to avoid repli-
cation. Security maintenance is a cat-and-mouse game; every patch of an
unauthorized hole in the firewall protecting sensitive information also
is a challenge to tricksters to find new means of entry. Each list establishes
a type of relationship (with donors, with reporters, with volunteers) that a
campaign must nurse with emotional as well as quantitative intelligence.

In short, the ineluctable dynamism of online campaigning requires its practitioners to put a price on the services they offer that will make their businesses viable, if not wildly profitable.

When dot-pols get a handle on these three qualities, online campaigning will be a full partner in the campaign profession. Trial and error will then occur in the context of accepted practices. As these practices dovetail with those in polling, television, direct mail, and so forth, the distinction between online and other forms of media will disappear. Then, one of these days, an Internet campaigner will get credit for a victory. The credit will start within the professional political community, as success leads to a swelled client roster. Then that campaigner's opposite numbers will gain more clients on the argument that they alone can make their side competitive. The press will get wind at some point, and the feature writers will make the star look like an overnight sensation. But that will be the end of the story, really, not the beginning.

Joe Trippi, a dot-com marketing consultant who returned to politics to manage the Dean campaign, may be the first dot-pol star, with Zephyr Teachout, the online organizer, and Matthew Gross, the head blogger, in supporting roles. The Dean campaign has demonstrated the right attitude for online campaigning. It tinkers constantly and is swift to correct and apologize for mistakes. For example, Gross responded to spamming complaints in mid-August 2003 by apologizing and severing relations with two vendors found responsible. Like MoveOn, the Dean campaign also sets short-term fund-raising and list-building goals that it has thus far been able to meet or surpass, creating bursts of news coverage and expressions of "We did it!" enthusiasm among the blogging faithful. The campaign's embrace of MeetUp may be its greatest innovation. Holding monthly meetings gives the online grassroots network its equivalent of the church basement, union hall, and board room: a place where solidarity can grow and ripen into coordinated action.

WHEN THINGS REALLY GET "CYBER"

With today's equipment and knowledge, a campaign console can be built, the seat before it can be occupied, and a political network can be humming. But there is more in store technologically. Part of what is to come revolves around the original meaning of the word "cybernetics." The cyber- prefix has become synonymous with the Internet, but it derives from advances in communication theory dating back to the 1940s.[13] Roughly put, cybernetics refers to the capacity of computers to fine-tune outputs automatically on the basis of recent inputs. A political professional employing cybernetics would run a database operation—say, the Election Day rank ordering of precincts to be canvassed by campaign volunteers—such that the order would change in keeping with early results. A cybernetic program can provide a campaign strategist with exceedingly timely intelligence so long as three conditions obtain: (1) something can be tabulated (voters showing up at local polling stations), (2) a benchmark number can be assigned to each category in which the thing is to be counted (turnout by precinct in the last comparable election),[14] and (3) a value can be assigned to the difference between the incoming counts and the benchmark numbers (for example, the bigger the expected/actual gap, the more important canvassing is, and so the higher on the list the precinct should be). In this example, the allocation of a scarce resource (the canvassers) can be optimized on the fly. In general, as political scientist Karl Deutsch put it:

> If the feedback is well-designed, the result will be a series of diminishing mistakes—a dwindling series of over- and under-corrections converging on the goal. If the functioning of the feedback or servomechanism is not adequate to its task . . . the mistakes may become greater. The network may be "hunting" over a cyclical or widening range of tentative and "incorrect" responses, ending in a breakdown of the mechanism.[15]

Computer-tabulated and Internet data can be read manually as well. Defenders of Wildlife, an environmental advocacy organization, was one of the first campaigns to rely on such feedback. Working with the subscriber base of the Juno Advocacy Network, a collection of Internet users who agreed to participate in tests and surveys in exchange for free access, Defenders of Wildlife tested two recruiting messages on 50,000 subscribers each. A message on endangered species yielded a 9 percent response, while one on endangered wolves in Yellowstone Park attracted an 11 percent return. The group promptly rolled out the wolves message to the entire subscriber base of 500,000.[16]

The manual method is actually preferable from a dot-pol's point of view. If, as in polling, a consultant must interpret the data, then there are repeated opportunities to earn a fee and commissions from a campaign. But a campaign that installed a cybernetic system would pay the

Internet consultant a onetime fee. That may help explain why the cybernetic capacities of networked computers have scarcely been tapped in online politics to date. When they are, a classic computer-human dilemma will be updated: should a campaign go with the adjustments the cybernetic system stipulates or with what the person or various people at the console think and believe? The horns of the dilemma will be gnarlier whenever the goal of the database operation appears fuzzy to the data consumer. What if a console reader has forgotten, or never knew, whether the parameters on which the numbers are being adjusted were set as part of a popularity contest or a poll? The campaign could be led astray. Whatever the outcome and degree of automation, instantaneous incorporation of feedback is coming. "Look for mid-course corrections on the teleprompter," scholar Arthur Isak Applbaum predicted.[17]

SETTLING INTO MATURITY

Slow as it seems, the transitional period for online campaigning will not last forever. When it concludes, patterns of online behavior in public life will largely be set for a generation. In some respects, the distinction between "online" and traditional media will have vanished thanks to "convergence" devices that allow interchangeable access to the Net, the phone system, television and radio networks, and other media. What I have referred to as a "digital political machine" will have its own moniker, much as "horseless carriages" turned into automobiles, and "flying machines" into airplanes. People will go to this technically enhanced and more orderly Net as a matter of habit, to find out more about political messages they may have heard about on the radio, glimpsed on a billboard, or even anticipated in their own minds. Who is running for what offices, pushing what legislation? Where do they stand in relation to each other? Who is working for them? What can we do? People will come to expect that answers to these and other basic questions about politics will be found online.

The transition period for online campaigning also is a period freighted with significance for those concerned about the civic quality of politics. The dot-pols and their counterparts in professional politics will have a say, but so will legislators, regulators, judges, and the executives and lobbyists of the major dot-com companies. What about the occasional participants, the voters and "extras"?

The optimal time to ensure free and universal access to certain types of campaign material is before, not after, pricing protocols harden in the politics profession and online advertising industry. Once organizations start counting on paid political messages for regular revenue, they will oppose efforts to make it freely available. The example with cable television is at once instructive and cautionary: the cable industry provided for C-SPAN while it still needed public approval and government protections. Had Brian Lamb developed C-SPAN after the industry won state protections, the outcome might have been different. The broadband industry will follow the same pattern.

Since the Internet is a multidirectional medium, "access" takes on extra meanings. Different public access standards may apply with respect to viewing, publishing, sharing, and modifying campaign items. In some respects, however, the Internet can be configured much the same as other media. For instance, the distinction between commercial and noncommercial content can be readily and justifiably transposed into cyberspace.

Lovers of liberal, democratic, and republican politics (in which individuals freely monitor events, discuss policy, and exercise critical powers over government officials, under law) should work to see that online campaigning can revive something of the personal web of relationships characteristic of politicians during the heyday of political party machines. Robert Putnam put his finger on the big problem with American campaign politics today: "Financial capital—the wherewithal for mass marketing—has steadily replaced social capital—that is, grassroots citizen networks—as the coin of the realm."[18] The power of the technique embraced by Andy Brack, to walk the streets and meet constituents face to face, was greatly diminished during the mass media era. To push for its revival is not to hope for a return to the nineteenth century: the party era also was one of rampant discrimination and corruption.

The Internet is not likely to resocialize politics. Cyberspace cannot house the new public square. However, online campaigners can fill the gaps between direct contacts among political players far better than the mass media. It is perfect for organizing meetings and providing background information and personal reminders to motivate people to attend. Networked political institutions can rejuvenate civic participation, not on a mass scale but at a level where fans of the political spectacle can become "extras," both at their own behest and in response to campaign appeals.

For their part, online campaigners, should learn to manage human networks as well as to develop texts and Web sites. They should take full advantage of Net telephony—should the telecommunications powers that be allow it to flourish—since political persuasion is, in essence, an oral art. Expanding civic participation through the Internet can be salutary. The Net may not become the most trafficked or talked-about channel for political communication (TV seems the champ), nor the most persuasive channel (there is no way to twist an arm through fiber-optic cable), but it may well become the control center for politicking in the next few years.

All politics is still local, in the sense that big decisions of strategy and policy are still likely to be hammered out among a few people inside a single room, where they can bargain, intimidate, and compromise. Television continues to shape the environment in which local politics occurs; if something is not on television, it is not perceived as real by most people. Nevertheless, in the future all winning campaigns will have a grounding in broadband communications. The Internet has altered the best ways in which to build networks of people and databases of knowledge about donors and activists, the opposition, policy details, the media, and so on. No computerized network, no reaching the potential of people power. No computerized databases, no exploiting the effectiveness of pattern recognition.

The coming centrality of online campaigning to politics means we need to set high standards of behavior for online campaigning and to find ways of publicizing and enforcing them. If we succeed, our democratic ideals will continue to be within sight, if not always within our grasp.

Notes

PREFACE

1. Campaign Finance Institute, "Large Donors Dominate Presidential Fundraising for First 9 Months," news release, October 17, 2003 (updated October 23, 2003), www.cfinst.org .

2. "We are all 'occasional' politicians when we cast our ballot or consummate a similar expression of intention, such as applauding or protesting in a 'political' meeting, or delivering a 'political' speech, etc. . . . There are two ways of making politics one's vocation: either one lives 'for' politics or one lives 'off' politics. By no means is this contrast an exclusive one. The rule is rather, that man does both, at least in thought, and certainly he also does both in practice." Max Weber, "Politics as a Vocation," in Hans H. Gerth and C. Wright Mills, eds., *From Max Weber: Essays in Sociology* (New York: Oxford University Press, 1946), pp. 83–84.

3. Hugh Heclo, "Campaigning and Governing: A Conspectus," in Norman Ornstein and Thomas Mann, eds., *The Permanent Campaign and Its Future* (Washington, D.C.: AEI Press, 2000).

4. James A. Thurber, Candice J. Nelson, and David A. Dulio, "Portrait of Campaign Consultants," in James A. Thurber and Candice J. Nelson, eds., *Campaign Warriors: Political Consultants in Elections* (Washington, D.C.: Brookings Institution Press, 2000).

5. Ruth Marcus, "Costliest Race Nears End; Bush, Gore Running Close; U.S. Campaigns Fuel $3 Billion in Spending," *Washington Post,* November 6, 2000. Campaign professionals receive an indeterminate fraction of this total. In television advertising, for example, which soaks up roughly 33–40 percent of election campaign spending, consultants usually receive 15 percent of the amount spent on placing the ads.

6. The estimate comes from Mike McCurry, a press secretary to President Clinton who became chief executive officer of a leading online politics firm, Grassroots.com, in late 2000. Rebecca Fairley Raney, "With the Polls

Closed, Political Sites Seek a New Focus," *New York Times,* November 27, 2000.

7. Dennis W. Johnson, "The Business of Political Consulting," in Thurber and Nelson, *Campaign Warriors,* p. 43.

8. Richard F. Fenno, Jr., *Watching Politicians: Essays on Participant Observation* (Berkeley, Calif.: Institute of Governmental Studies Press, 1990); Anthony King, *Running Scared: Why America's Politicians Campaign Too Much and Govern Too Little* (New York: Free Press, 1996); Ornstein and Mann, *Permanent Campaign and Its Future;* Larry J. Sabato, *The Rise of Political Consultants: New Ways of Winning Elections* (New York: Basic Books, 1981); Thurber and Nelson, *Campaign Warriors.*

9. The estimate comes from Philip Howard, a graduate student at Northwestern University completing an ethnographic study of the online politics community, in personal correspondence with the author, February 5, 2001. Of course, election day in a presidential year marks a peak. A better number may be 766, the number of different people who had attended a major e-politics conference from a list of thirty such events since 1995.

CHAPTER 1

1. A similar initiative appeared in the United Kingdom in the spring of 2001, offering to match Liberal Democrats and Laborites so that the ranks of Conservative M.P.s would be held to a minimum. See Tactical Voter's site online at www.tacticalvoter.net.

2. "A Republican-Democratic Cyberwar," www.usatoday.com, November 7, 2000; Jay Lyman, "Hackers Make Mark on Presidential Race," NewsFactor Network, November 8, 2000, available online at www.newsfactor.com /perl/story/4781.html.

3. Mark Jurkowitz, "One E-mail Starts Anti-Gore Storm," *Boston Globe,* November 18, 2000.

4. Tracy Westen, "Can Technology Save Democracy?" *National Civic Review* 87, no. 1 (Spring 1998): 48.

5. For concise accounts, see Bruce C. Klopfenstein, "The Internet Phenomenon," and David H. Goff, "Issues of Internet Infrastructure," in Alan B. Albarran and David H. Goff, eds., *Understanding the Web: Social, Political, and Economic Dimensions of the Internet* (Ames, Iowa: Iowa State University Press, 2000).

6. For a good history of the early years of online campaigning, see Graeme Browning, *Electronic Democracy: Using the Internet to Transform*

American Politics, 2nd edition (Medford, N.J.: Information Today, Inc., 2002). The Communications Decency Act was subsequently declared unconstitutional by a federal court.

7. A continuing list of firsts in online politics may be viewed online at www.politicsonline.com.

8. Howard Fineman, "Pressing the Flesh On-line," *Newsweek,* October 20, 1999.

9. Thanks to Pam Fielding for the one-liner. The great exception to the prediction rule is, of course, JFK's 1961 declaration that the United States would put a man on the moon by the end of the decade.

10. That said, eighty-four Americans actually cast online ballots in November 2000, under the aegis of the Federal Voting Assistance Program. Five counties, including two in Florida, participated in this pilot program for absentee voters. The votes were encrypted, authenticated by digital signatures, accompanied by paper ballots, and routed through Defense Department computers. Brady Snyder, "14 in Weber Help Pilot Net Vote," *Deseret News,* November 15, 2000.

11. Michael Margolis and David Resnick, *Politics as Usual: The Cyberspace "Revolution"* (Thousand Oaks, Calif.: Sage Publications, 2000).

12. Michael Cornfield, Lee Rainie, and John B. Horrigan, "Untuned Keyboards: Online Campaigners, Citizens, and Portals in the 2002 Elections," Institute for Politics, Democracy, and the Internet, Graduate School of Political Management, George Washington University, March 21, 2003, pp. 14–16, available online at http://www.ipdi.org/untuned.pdf or www.pewinternet.org.

13. These numbers are drawn from surveys conducted by Princeton Survey Research Associates for the Pew Research Center for the People and the Press; the Pew Internet and American Life Project, Pew Research Center; and the Institute for Politics, Democracy, and the Internet, Graduate School of Political Management, George Washington University, available online at http://people-press.org, www.pewinternet.org, or www.ipdi.org.

14. In *Campaigning Online* (New York: Oxford University Press, 2003), political scientists Bruce Bimber and Richard Davis show empirically that civic and campaign Web sites in 2000 had minimal effects on voters. Their research did not examine possible effects registered throughout the rest of the Internet.

CHAPTER 2

1. "How Americans Used the Internet after the Terror Attack," Pew Internet and American Life Project, Pew Research Center, Washington, D.C.,

September 15, 2001, available online at www.pewinternet.org/reports/pdfs/PIP_Terror_Report.pdf.

2. According to data at Search Engine Watch, available online at www.searchenginewatch.com.

3. "Counting on the Internet," Pew Internet and American Life Project, Pew Research Center, Washington, D.C., December 29, 2002, available online at www.pewinternet.org/reports/pdfs/PIP_Expectations.pdf.

4. There were, to be sure, political information sites that charged access fees, too: for example, www.wsj.com, the online version of the *Wall Street Journal,* and www.campaignstudygroup.com (now defunct), put forth by the Campaign Study Group of Springfield, Va., which deconstructs campaign finance information.

5. In *Next: The Future Just Happened* (New York: W. W. Norton, 2001), Michael Lewis tells stories about such revolutionary individuals, including children in some cases.

6. Steven Pinker, *How The Mind Works* (New York: W. W. Norton, 1997), pp. 60–69.

7. Michael Cornfield, Lee Rainie, and John B. Horrigan, "Untuned Keyboards: Online Campaigners, Citizens, and Portals in the 2002 Elections," Institute for Politics, Democracy, and the Internet, Graduate School of Political Management, George Washington University, March 21, 2003, p. 17, available online at http://www.ipdi.org/untuned.pdf or www.pewinternet.org.

8. National Election Studies, Center for Political Studies, University of Michigan, "NES Guide to Public Opinion and Electoral Behavior," Tables 2a.1 and 2a.2, available online at www.umich.edu/~nes.

9. Dennis W. Johnson, *Clogged Circuits: Congress, Communications, and the Internet* (New York: Routledge, forthcoming).

10. Which is not to say that a progressive agenda is perennially doomed, any more so than to claim that it would be enacted with a revolution of smart extras. There are progressive professionals and nonprogressive smart voters.

11. Tom Price, *Cyber Activism: Advocacy Groups and the Internet,* Foundation for Public Affairs, Washington, D.C., 2000, p. 11.

12. Albert L. May, *The Virtual Trail: Political Journalism on the Internet,* Institute for Politics, Democracy, and the Internet, Graduate School of Political Management, George Washington University, 2002, available online at http://www.ipdi.org/virtual_trail.pdf.

13. David Brauer, "Wordgate: Is Minnesota Sen. Rod Grams Running a Cyber-Dirty-Tricks Campaign?" *Slate,* July 21, 2000, available online at http://slate.msn.com/id/86798/.

14. Patrick Ball et al., "Killings and Refugee Flow in Kosovo, March-June 1999: A Report to the International Criminal Tribunal for the Former Yugoslavia," American Association for the Advancement of Science and American Bar Association Central and East European Law Initiative, Washington, D.C., January 3, 2002, available online at http://shr.aaas.org/kosovo/icty_report.pdf.

15. Gail Collins, *Scorpion Tongues: Gossip, Celebrity, and American Politics* (New York: William Morrow, 1998).

16. Mancur Olson, Jr., *The Logic of Collective Action: Public Goods and the Theory of Groups* (Cambridge, Mass.: Harvard University Press, 1965), p. 2.

17. Arthur Lupia and Gisela Sin, "Which Public Goods Are Endangered? How Evolving Communication Technologies Affect *The Logic of Collective Action*," *Public Choice*, forthcoming, available online at www.personal.umich.edu/~lupia/olson.pdf.

18. A nonattitude is an answer to a survey question that does not reflect a genuine attitude on the part of the respondent. Nonattitudes arise out of a poll respondent's desire to not seem ignorant or uncooperative. Nonattitudes are one kind of measurement error: an accurate account of misleading information. Whereas sampling errors can be statistically estimated, measurement errors render opinion surveys into matters of opinion.

19. Michael Cornfield, "Adding In the Net: Making Citizenship Count in the Digital Age," in David M. Anderson and Michael Cornfield, eds., *The Civic Web: Online Politics and Democratic Values* (Lanham, Md.: Rowman and Littlefield, 2002), p. 97–112.

20. See the December 6, 1999, poll commissioned by the Democracy Online Project (now the Institute for Politics, Democracy, and the Internet, Graduate School of Political Management, George Washington University), executive summary available online at http://www.democracyonline.org/dec6survey.shtml. The online public wants voting records and ties its judgments regarding credibility and trust to the opportunity to check facts.

CHAPTER THREE

1. Campaign Web sites, the topic of this chapter, should not be confused with the "—.gov" Web sites of public officials and government bodies. Those have as their main purposes the delivery of government services and—critical for democratic values—the provision of forums for public comment

on those services and for public contribution to policy deliberations. Campaign Web sites are purely political constructions, and they have as their identifying markers a "—.com" domain address and a disclaimer at the bottom of the home page declaring them to be paid for by a particular campaign organization.

2. "Modest Increase in Internet Use for Campaign 2002," news release, Pew Research Center for the People and the Press, Washington, D.C., January 5, 2003, available at http://people-press.org. Other choices were offered, and multiple responses were accepted, notwithstanding the phrase "most often."

3. A survey conducted by the Republican polling firm Market Strategies in July 2000 found that 40 percent of registered voters occasionally opened unsolicited e-mail; about 9 percent of them said they had received unsolicited e-mail from political sources. "A Profile of the On-line U.S. Electorate," Market Strategies, Livonia, Mich., August 22, 2000.

4. John Mintz, "Political Groups Scramble to Find E-Mail Addresses of Likely Backers," *Washington Post,* October 22, 2000.

5. On the history and virtues of federalized advocacy groups, see Theda Skocpol, "Advocates without Members: The Recent Transformation of American Civic Life," in Theda Skocpol and Morris P. Fiorina, eds., *Civic Engagement in American Democracy* (Washington, D.C.: Brookings Institution Press/Russell Sage Foundation, 1999).

6. Daron R. Shaw, "How the Bush and Gore Campaigns Conceptualized and Used the Internet in 2000," *Journal of Political Marketing* 1, no. 1 (Spring 2002): 61.

7. Ibid., p. 59.

8. Bob Davis and Jeanne Cummings, "Hot Buttons: A Barrage of E-Mail Helps Candidates Hit Media Fast and Often," *Wall Street Journal,* September 21, 2000.

9. Studies of campaign e-mail are on the academic horizon.

10. Research by Pam Fielding of the consulting firm e-advocates, with the involvement of Juno Online Services. The Web-savvy challengers who won contests classified as toss-ups: Mike Ross (Arkansas 4th district), Adam Schiff (California 27th), Jane Harman (California 36th), Susan Davis (California 49th), Thomas Carper (Delaware Senate), and—the only challenger in this group who also outspent the incumbent—George Allen (Virginia Senate). The results did not include the Cantwell-Gorton contest, for it was undecided at the time of the news release (November 13, 2000). Both of those candidates for the Washington Senate seat did equally well by Fielding's criteria.

CHAPTER 4

1. For example, see Glenn R. Simpson, "Bush Launches an Internet Advertising Campaign," *Wall Street Journal,* December 21, 1999.
2. Leo Bogart, *Commercial Culture: The Media System and the Public Interest,* (New York: Oxford University Press, 1995), p. 16.
3. "Electing Not to Advertise: Campaigning on the Web," intelligence report, AdRelevance Intelligence, October 2000, available online at www.adrelevance.com/intelligence/intel_report_001030.pdf.
4. Mitch Johnson, manager, mid-Atlantic regional sales, 24/7 Media, speaking at an E-Voter Institute Conference, Washington, D.C., January 17, 2001. A poll conducted by the institute one year later, surveying 411 "political and advocacy communication leaders," found that more than half of them (56 percent) did not recommend online advertising to their clients. No other Net utility received as high a nonendorsement. By comparison, only 15 percent had not recommended developing a Web site or collecting e-mail addresses. "Dawning of a New Era: Measuring the Initial Impact of the Internet on Political and Advocacy Communication," E-Voter Institute, Washington, D.C., December 2001, executive summary available online at http://www.e-voterinstitute.com/docs/evi.sp.e.2001.html.
5. One of them, Cyrus Krohn, wrote about it for his publication. Cyrus Krohn, "On-line Political Advertising: Our Salesman Reports," *Slate,* September 22, 1999, available online at http://slate.msn.com/id/35246/.
6. An impression is an appearance on a computer screen somewhere, probably before one person, also known as "a pair of eyeballs" but not necessarily a unique person; the same ad flashed on two occasions on one computer's screen counts as two impressions. The DNC's fall 2000 ad buy was for 8.1 million impressions, while the RNC's was for 9.4 million. See "Electing Not to Advertise." Most online ad buys last until the number of impressions is reached, although buys for a particular time period and by-the-click are possible as well.
7. Author's interview with Ben Green of the Gore campaign, January 12, 2001.
8. Hugh Carter Donahue, "The Philadelphia Mayoral Election of 1999: Findings and Observations," paper written for the Democracy Online Project (now the Institute for Politics, Democracy, and the Internet, Graduate School of Political Management, George Washington University), January 2000.
9. Author's interview with Andrew Brack, March 2, 2001.

10. Lauren Weinstein, "Web Tracking and Data Matching Hit the Campaign Trail," *Privacy Forum Digest* 8, no. 22 (December 23, 1999), available online at www.vortex.com/privacy/priv.08.22.

11. Leslie Wayne, "Voter Profiles Selling Briskly as Privacy Issues Are Raised," *New York Times,* September 9, 2000.

12. Harlan Lebo, "Surveying the Digital Future: The UCLA Internet Report," Center for Communication Policy, University of California, Los Angeles, October 25, 2000, available online at www.ccp.ucla.edu/UCLA-Internet-Report-2000.pdf.

13. "Privacy Concerns and Its Effects on Americans Online," Democracy Online Project (now the Institute for Politics, Democracy, and the Internet, Graduate School of Political Management, George Washington University), November 2001, available online at www.ipdi.org/2001SurveyAnalysis.pdf.

14. "Work Trends V: Nothing but Net: American Workers and the Information Economy: Americans' Attitudes about Work, Employers and Government," John J. Heldrich Center for Workforce Development, Rutgers University, and Center for Survey Research and Analysis, University of Connecticut, February 2000, available online at www.heldrich.rutgers.edu/Resources/Publication/41/NothingButNet.pdf.

15. For an example of what this kind of data entails, see the Media Audit Web site, available online at www.themediaaudit.com.

16. The agency Dynamic Logic has proffered research showing, it said, that returns on investment peaked with five exposures to an online ad. *Beyond the Click* (Dynamic Logic, New York), June 2001, www.dynamiclogic.com/beyond_1_8.php. This kind of rule was lacking in 2000 and has yet to be adopted as an industry standard.

17. Michael Schudson, *Advertising, the Uneasy Persuasion: Its Dubious Impact on American Society* (New York: Basic Books, 1984), p. 4.

18. Seth Godin, a freelance author and self-described "agent of change" for the advertising industry, in a speech before an E-Voter Institute conference, Washington, D.C., January 17, 2001. His book on the topic is Seth Godin, *Permission Marketing: Turning Strangers into Friends, and Friends into Customers* (New York: Simon and Schuster, 1999).

19. Saul Hansell, "Marketers Find Internet Opens New Avenues to Customers," *New York Times,* March 26, 2001.

20. Karen A. B. Jagoda et al., "Measuring the Effectiveness of the Internet in Election 2000," E-Voter Institute, Washington, D.C., January 2001.

21. Author's interview with Jonah Seiger, March 16, 2001. This paragraph also is informed by a presentation by Charles Warner, vice president of interactive marketing, America Online, Washington, D.C., June 19, 2001.

22. "DoubleClick Offers Improved Way to Target Email Ads," *Yahoo! News*, February 25, 2002.

23. Kay Lehman Schlozman, Sidney Verba, and Henry E. Brady, "Civic Participation and the Equality Problem," in Theda Skocpol and Morris P. Fiorina, eds., *Civic Engagement in American Democracy* (Washington, D.C.: Brookings Institution Press/Russell Sage Foundation, 1999).

24. Robert Schlesinger, "Electronic Politics: Political Fund-raising Comes into Its Own on the World Wide Web," *Roll Call*, October 27, 1999.

25. Ryan Thornburg, "Digital Donors: How Campaigns Are Using the Internet to Raise Money and How It's Affecting Democracy," occasional paper, Democracy Online Project (now the Institute for Politics, Democracy, and the Internet, Graduate School of Political Management, George Washington University), November 2001.

26. News release, eContributor.com, Washington, D.C., September 6, 2001.

27. In 2000, a mere eight hundred donors accounted for approximately $300 million of the $487 million raised and spent in soft money. Thomas E. Mann, "Lessons for Reformers," in David B. Magleby, ed., *Financing the 2000 Election* (Washington, D.C.: Brookings Institution Press, 2002).

28. At the turn of the millennium, according to a survey of 2,200 candidates running for U.S. office at every level of government, 23 percent of them spent more than half of their personal schedule on fund-raising. More than half (55 percent) devoted at least a quarter of their time to the money chase. Peter L. Francia and Paul S. Herrnson, "Begging for Bucks," *Campaigns and Elections* (Votenet, Washington, D.C.), April 2001, p. 51.

CHAPTER 5

1. Wesley Dale Wilson, "A Different Kind of e-publican: An Analysis and Critique of the 2000 Presidential eCampaign of George W. Bush," University of Texas master's thesis, May 2001, p. 6, available online at www.wesleywilson.com/pr/wesleywilson_pr.pdf.

2. Ibid.

3. Author's interview with Tucker Eskew of the Bush campaign, February 9, 2001.

4. Wilson, "Different Kind of e-publican," p. 10.

5. As well as the campaigns did linking Web content to a television event, someone named Basil Valentine with a Yahoo e-mail address did them one better. His "The 2000 Presidential Debates Drinking Game" made the e-mail rounds on the days before the first debate. "2 drinks if Gore reminisces about his

hardscrabble upbringing on a Tennessee farm." "1 drink if Bush looks at 'The Big Picture.'" And so forth.

6. Wilson, "Different Kind of e-publican," p. 29.

7. This chapter is based on the author's interviews and conversations with Max Fose and Dan Schnur of the McCain campaign, as well as research conducted by two graduate students, Alex Storey and Erin Hickman.

8. Steve Davis, Larry Elin, and Grant Reeher, *Click on Democracy: The Internet's Power to Change Political Apathy into Civic Action* (Boulder, Colo.: Westview Press, 2002), p. 57.

9. These contribution figures were publicly challenged. Critics contended that the McCain campaign padded the numbers by directing donors contacted through other media to the Internet.

10. For balanced accounts of the Ventura campaign and the role of the Internet, see David Beiler, "The Body Politic Registers a Protest," *Campaigns and Elections* (Votenet, Washington, D.C.), February 1999; Jon Jeter, "Campaign Reform Helped 'The Body' Slam Rivals," *Washington Post*, November 5, 1998; Rebecca Fairley Raney, "Former Wrestler's Campaign Got a Boost from the Internet," *New York Times*, November 6, 1998.

11. Phillip Matier and Andrew Ross, "Ammiano Emerges in S.F.'s Election of Discontent," *San Francisco Chronicle*, November 3, 1999. Cited in Rhett Francisco, "Has The Internet Been An Effective Campaign Tool for Local Candidates?" unpublished senior thesis, Claremont McKenna College, 2001.

12. Soon after the McCain campaign noticed from its log files that representatives from the Bush campaign visited frequently, "Bush buttons" popped up to inform visitors that the page they were on was a favorite of the Texan's team.

13. Ed Schwartz, *NetActivism: How Citizens Use the Internet* (Sebastopol, Calif.: O'Reilly and Associates, Inc., 1996).

14. David Barnhizer, "Environmental Activism on the Internet," in Steven Hick and John G. McNutt, eds., *Advocacy, Activism, and the Internet: Community Organization and Social Policy* (Chicago: Lyceum Books, 2002), pp. 95–111.

15. Full text available on Nobel Foundation website, online at www.nobel.se/peace/laureates/1997/presentation-speech.html.

16. Jody Williams, "Politics Unusual: A Different Model of International Cooperation," International Campaign to Ban Landmines, Washington, D.C., 2000, available online at http://www.icbl.org/amb/williams/politics_unusual.html.

17. Michael Cornfield, "The Watergate Audience: Parsing the Powers of the Press," in James W. Carey, ed., *Media, Myths, and Narratives: Television*

and the Press (Newbury Park, Calif.: Sage Publications, 1988), p. 195. Earlier in the crime story news narrative, Nixon aide Alexander Haig used the word "firestorm," with its nuclear blast connotations, to characterize the adverse and comparably spontaneous public reaction to the firing of Archibald Cox, an independent special prosecutor appointed by the Nixon administration to investigate the Watergate scandal, and the concomitant double resignation of Attorney General Elliot Richardson and his second, William Ruckelshaus. This framing of presidential action as a "Saturday Night Massacre" (a term taken from the gangster era) and public reaction as a firestorm forced Nixon to name another special prosecutor and turn over Oval Office tapes to John Sirica, the federal judge presiding over the trial of the Watergate burglars.

18. Daniel Bennett and Pam Fielding, *The Net Effect: How Cyberadvocacy Is Changing the Political Landscape* (Merrifield, Va.: Capitol Advantage Publishing, 1999), p. 21.

19. For more about innovative uses of the Internet by protest movements, see the work of W. Lance Bennett at http://depts.washington.edu/gcp/research _pages/global_activist_networks.htm.

20. Data as compiled by the opensecrets.org Web site of the Center for Responsive Politics, Washington, D.C., 2003, available online at www. opensecrets.org.

21. The Markle Foundation contracted with the author to assist with their internal evaluation of Web White and Blue 2000. The analysis here is based on the work done for them.

22. Ronald A. Faucheux, "Nationwide Poll: What Voters Think About Candidate Debates," in Ronald A. Faucheux, ed., *The Debate Book* (Washington, D.C.: Campaigns and Elections Publishing, 2003), p. 87.

23. Anthony J. Eksterowicz and Robert N. Roberts, eds., *Public Journalism and Political Knowledge* (Lanham, Md.: Rowman and Littlefield, 2000).

24. Author's interview with Ron Howard and Josh King, speakout.com, October 23, 2000.

25. "Mistakes, Exaggeration Mark Media Use of Focus Groups on Presidential Debate" and "AAPOR Did Not Intend to Criticize NBC and MSNBC for Their Overall Use of a Group of Undecided Voters," press releases, American Association for Public Opinion Research, Lenexa, Kansas, October 16 and October 20, 2000, available online at www.aapor .org/default.asp?ID=10&.page=news_and_issues/press_releases _and_official_statements. The second release pulled back on the criticism.

26. Dick Morris, *Behind the Oval Office: Getting Reelected Against All Odds*, 2d ed. (Los Angeles: Renaissance Books, 1999).

27. If you thought this endnote might be the print equivalent of a click-through, you are correct. Of 29,822 "votes" cast, 84 percent agreed with the premise of the question and the statement "It's time for them to step back and let Gore step to the forefront of the Democratic Party," while the remaining 16 percent agreed that "their efforts are building excitement for the vice president's campaign." See the vote.com Web site, available online at www.vote.com.

28. Michael Cornfield, Lee Rainie, and John B. Horrigan, "Untuned Keyboards: Online Campaigners, Citizens, and Portals in the 2002 Elections," Institute for Politics, Democracy, and the Internet, Graduate School of Political Management, George Washington University, March 21, 2003, pp. 20–21, available online at http://www.ipdi.org/untuned.pdf or www.pewinternet.org.

29. Ibid., p. 6.

30. Jeffrey B. Abramson, F. Christopher Arterton, and Gary R. Orren, *The Electronic Commonwealth: The Impact of New Media Technologies on Democratic Politics* (New York: Basic Books, 1988); Lawrence K. Grossman, *The Electronic Republic: Reshaping Democracy in the Information Age* (New York: Viking, 1995).

31. See the frequently asked questions section on the Google News page, available online at www.google.com/help/about_news_search.html.

32. Dick Morris, *Vote.com: How Big-Money Lobbyists and the Media Are Losing Their Influence and the Internet Is Giving Power to the People* (New York: St. Martin's Press, 1999), p. 28.

33. Susan Herbst, *Numbered Voices: How Opinion Polling Has Shaped American Politics* (Chicago: University of Chicago Press, 1993), p. 166.

34. Howard Kurtz, "Who Wants to Be the President? Politics to Meet Reality TV on Cable's 'American Candidate,'" *Washington Post*, February 17, 2003.

35. Michael Lewis, "The Two-Bucks-a-Minute Democracy," *New York Times Magazine*, November 5, 2000, pp. 64–67.

CHAPTER 6

1. Langdon Winner, "The Internet and Dreams of Democratic Renewal," in David M. Anderson and Michael Cornfield, eds., *The Civic Web: Online Politics and Democratic Values* (Lanham, Md.: Rowman and Littlefield, 2002).

2. Wayne Rash, Jr., *Politics on the Nets: Wiring the Political Process* (New York: W. H. Freeman, 1997), p. 80.

3. Ibid., p. 170.

4. Jon Katz, "Digital Citizens," *Wired,* December 1997.

5. Ed Keller and Jon Berry, *The Influentials* (New York: Free Press, 2003), p. 38.

6. Richard Davis, *The Web of Politics: The Internet's Impact on the American Political System* (New York: Oxford University Press, 1999), p. 5.

7. Michael Margolis and David Resnick, *Politics as Usual: The Cyberspace "Revolution"* (Thousand Oaks Calif.: Sage Publications, 2000), p. 72–73.

8. Bruce Bimber, "The Internet and Political Transformation: Populism, Community, and Accelerated Pluralism," *Polity* 31, no. 1 (Fall 1998): 133–60.

9. Pippa Norris, *A Virtuous Circle: Political Communications in Postindustrial Societies* (New York: Cambridge University Press, 2000), p. 140.

10. There has been considerable policy debate and action regarding the Internet and pornography, but it is hard to see a change in the alliance of forces over the issue.

11. For more on trial runs and other processes critical to the social adoption of a new technology, see Everett M. Rogers, *Diffusion of Innovations,* 4th ed. (New York: Free Press, 1995).

12. Author's interview with John Beezer, January 3, 2000, Washington, D.C.

13. The bible of cybernetics is Norbert Wiener, *Cybernetics: or Control and Communication in the Animal and the Machine* (New York: John Wiley and Sons, 1948).

14. A comparable election has a similar roster of offices on the ballot. Thus, a midterm election should be compared with the previous midterm election, not with the intervening presidential election, because presidential contests bring out more people.

15. Karl W. Deutsch, *The Nerves of Government: Models of Political Communication and Control* (New York: Free Press, 1966), p. 89.

16. Roger Stone, "Case Studies: Using the Internet to Build Citizen Armies," *Campaigns and Elections* (Votenet, Washington, D.C.), April 2001, p. 48.

17. Arthur Isak Applbaum, "Failure in the Cybermarketplace of Ideas," in Elaine Ciulla Kamarck and Joseph S. Nye, Jr., eds., *Governance.com: Democracy in the Information Age* (Washington, D.C.: Brookings Institution Press, 2002).

18. Robert D. Putnam, *Bowling Alone: The Collapse and Revival of American Community* (New York: Simon and Schuster, 2000), p. 40. Putnam devoted

fourteen pages to a consideration of whether the Internet could be a coun-
terforce to the decades-long erosion of social networking across the United
States that was the core concern of the book. He concluded that it could
supplement the work of civic entrepreneurs but that there was no substitute
for face-to-face communication.

INDEX

Note: Page numbers followed by letters *f, n,* and *t* refer to figures, notes, and tables, respectively.

ABOUT THE AUTHOR

MICHAEL CORNFIELD is a member of the faculty at George Washington University's Graduate School of Political Management and director of research of the University's Institute for Politics Democracy and the Internet, formerly known as the Democracy Online Project. A political scientist specializing in the study of the media and American politics and campaign communication, he also has taught at the University of Virginia and the College of William and Mary. He is coeditor (with David M. Anderson) of *The Civic Web: Online Politics and Democratic Values* (2002).